Goods and Services Tax (GST)

Impact on the Indian Economy

Goods and Services Tax (GST)

Impact on the Indian Economy

Edited by

Dr. Anjali Agarwal

Department of Economics,
Motilal Nehru College (Evening),
University of Delhi, Delhi

New Century Publications
New Delhi, India

NEW CENTURY PUBLICATIONS
4852 / 24, 1st Floor,
Ansari Road, Daryaganj,
New Delhi – 110 002 (India)

Tel.: 011-4101 7798; 4358 7398; 98112 66355
E-mail: info@newcenturypublications.com

www.newcenturypublications.com

Editorial office:
4800 / 24, Bharat Ram Road,
Ansari Road, Daryaganj,
New Delhi – 110 002

UGC Sponsored National Conference on Goods and Services Tax: Impact on Indian Economy, March 18 to 19, 2016

Reprint: 2025

ISBN: **978-81-7708-435-1**

First Published: 2017

Published by New Century Publications and printed at Milan Enterprises, New Delhi.

Designs: Patch Creative Unit, New Delhi.

PRINTED IN INDIA

About the Book

National level goods and services tax (GST) is India's most ambitious indirect tax reform. Its objective is to levy a single uniform tax across India on goods and services. GST, as and when implemented, would replace a number of Central and State taxes, making India more of a national integrated market, and bring more producers into the tax net.

The current structure of taxes on goods and services is highly complex, leaky (riddled with exemptions), and characterized by a complicated rate structure. There are parallel systems of indirect taxation at the Central and State levels. Each of the systems needs to be reformed to eventually harmonize them.

The changeover to GST, it is claimed, would significantly contribute to the buoyancy of tax revenues, acceleration of growth, and generation of many positive externalities.

To facilitate the introduction of GST, the Lok Sabha passed the 122nd Constitutional Amendment—Goods and Services Tax Bill on May 6, 2015. Rajya Sabha passed the same Bill with 9 amendments on August 3, 2016. Lok Sabha passed the modified Bill on August 8, 2016, approving all the 9 amendments by the Rajya Sabha. Currently, the hope is that GST will be implemented from April 1, 2017.

The present edited volume contains 19 research articles (divided into 5 sub-themes or parts) authored by experts in the field of public finance. This volume scrutinizes GST from various points of view. GST has now been implemented in 160 countries and case studies have been provided in this volume for an effective comparison. The detailed impact of GST on consumer, businessman, government, individual sectors/industries and national growth, along with a comparative analysis of GST with current indirect taxes, has also been presented.

These contributions provide deep insights into various aspects of GST and would add, constructively, to the raging debate in the country on the implications of the game-changing tax reform.

About the Editor

Dr. Anjali Agarwal is Assistant Professor and the current teacher-in-charge, Department of Economics, Motilal Nehru College (Evening), University of Delhi, Delhi. She was the convenor of the National Conference on GST organized by her college and funded by the University Grants Commission (UGC), New Delhi. She holds M.A. and Ph.D. degrees in economics. She has a teaching experience of more than 16 years in Delhi University.

Dr. Agarwal has published research papers in various journals of repute. She has also attended and presented research papers at various national and international seminars and conferences.

Her areas of specialization include productivity measurement in organized manufacturing industries, inclusive growth and employment and efficiency analysis.

FOREWORD

The Indian tax system has been a matter of debate since long. Given the federal structure of the Indian polity, the success of any tax reform heavily depends on the co-operation between the Centre and the States. Thus, while there have been many attempts to overhaul the tax system, the progress has been rather slow. This is perhaps because the conflicts between Centre and States retard such policy reform. This could be appreciated in the context of the larger picture of economic reforms that have unfolded since 1991 in banking, insurance, stock markets and other financial institutions. Such reforms have been effected relatively fast. Tax reforms have, on the other hand, been quite slow.

GST is a hybrid tax because it involves both goods and services. This increases the complexity and also the range of stakeholder. While in a democratic set up, it might be an inevitable consequence, and perhaps a requirement, wherein it is necessary to debate from the point of view of all stakeholders; there is also a need to carefully dissect and analyze the debate. There are some serious concerns about GST and the kind of debate surrounding it. The literature on GST has been concentrating only on two aspects: the administrative convenience (ease of doing business) and the likely impact of GST on the Indian economy (1-2 percent additional growth).

First, it is counter-intuitive to argue that any tax, which is a withdrawal (from the circular flow income in the economy), should lead to a 1-2 percent increase in GDP. It is an injection that leads to a growth in the national income, while tax is a withdrawal. Second, 'ease of doing business' is a criterion for evaluating a tax from the point of view of businesses. Usually, when we evaluate a tax, it should be done from the point of view of the economy including all factors of production and all economic entities. In all the recent literature that is available, there is hardly any writing (let alone erudite writing) that even mentions about the principles of taxation that are supposed to be applied while introducing a tax. It is time that we delve into the literature on VAT or GST to read, understand and apply these basic principles while indulging in academic discourse.

The four standard principles of taxation are as under:

1. Supply of resources.
2. Efficiency.
3. Equity.
4. Administrative efficiency.

The first principle implies that taxes adversely affect the incentive to work because they diminish the remuneration or return that a factor of production gets (wages to labour; interest to the owners of capital; and profit to the entrepreneur). Thus, a tax has the effect of reducing the supply of resources. It is necessary to evaluate a tax from this point of view.

Second, when taxes are imposed on the wages and rental price of capital, the factor price ratio gets distorted. This leads to inefficient allocation of resources. There would be sub-optimal allocation of resources. This would adversely affect output. In the light of this, it is not clear how some of the writings claim that GST would lead to GDP growth.

Third, when a tax is imposed, it pinches various economic agents in different degrees. Certain taxes are progressive and some are regressive. We need to analyse this aspect and then design a tax. Even an ex-post analysis would do.

Finally, imposition of a tax involves some cost of collection. The lower the cost of collection, as a percentage of tax yield, the higher the administrative efficiency of a tax. This, therefore, is to be applied as a criterion from the point of view of the government that imposes the tax.

From the above, it is obvious that an evaluation of a new tax is akin to project appraisal. Evaluation of economic policy is very much a part of project evaluation. What we need is nothing short of such an approach.

The purpose of any edited volume with multiple authors is to provoke debate. I hope that my critical comments will correct the course of the debate. Any literature must, first and foremost, be based on theory. Otherwise, it would be of limited value. It should enrich the subject and not just be a ready-reckoner.

The volume as proposed contains a good selection of research articles—some of the articles are from reputed authors. The topics covered are representative.

I wish the best for this edited volume of research articles on GST.

Professor K.V. Bhanu Murthy
Professor, and Former Head and Dean,
Faculty of Commerce and Business,
Delhi School of Economics,
University of Delhi

July 24, 2016

Contents

Contributors

Dr. Sacchidananda Mukherjee	Associate Professor, National Institute of Public Finance and Policy (NIPFP), New Delhi.
Mandeep Kaur	Assistant Professor, Dyal Singh College, University of Delhi, Delhi.
Dr. Vibha Gupta	Assistant Professor, Lakshmibai College, University of Delhi, Delhi.
Dharmveer	Assistant Professor, Sri Ram College of Commerce, University of Delhi, Delhi.
Renu Verma	Assistant Professor, Sri Ram College of Commerce, University of Delhi, Delhi.
Jasmine Jha	GGDSD College, Panjab University.
Professor Arun Kumar	Formerly Professor of Economics, Jawaharlal Nehru University (JNU), New Delhi.
Professor Kamal Nayan Kabra	Malcolm Adiseshiah Chair Professor, Economics of Development and Decentralized Planning, ISS, New Delhi and formerly Professor of Economics, IIPA, New Delhi.
Nitish Kashyap	Assistant Professor, Department of Economics, Miranda House, University of Delhi, Delhi.Æ
Dr. Anjali Agarwal	Assistant Professor, Department of Economics, Motilal Nehru College (Evening), University of Delhi, Delhi.
Amogh Agarwal	Research Scholar, NSIT, University of Delhi, Delhi.
Prabhjote Gill	GGDSD College, Chandigarh.

Pooja Sharma	Assistant Professor, Department of Economics, Daulat Ram College, University of Delhi, Delhi.
Ujjwala Gupta	Daulat Ram College, University of Delhi.
Vanshita Agarwal	Daulat Ram College, University of Delhi.
Ashish Kumar Sedai	Assistant Professor, Department of Economics, Kamala Nehru College, University of Delhi, Delhi.
Aashita Joshi	Department of Economics, Kamala Nehru College, University of Delhi, Delhi.
Saurabh Jain	Chartered Accountant
Priti Jain	Company Secretary
Dr. Sanjiv RanjanA	Assistant Professor, Motilal Nehru College (Evening), University of Delhi, Delhi.
Shashi Sawhney	Chartered Accountant
Dr. Vichitra Gupta	Associate Professor, Department of Political Science, Motilal Nehru College (Evening), University of Delhi, Delhi.
Professor Suresh Kumar	Head, Department of African Studies, University of Delhi, Delhi.
Dr. Prahlad Kumar Bairwa	Assistant Professor, Department of Political Science, Motilal Nehru College (Evening), University of Delhi, Delhi.
Dr. Premakumara G.S.	Faculty of Economics and UGC Research Awardee, Sir M.V. PG Centre (University of Mysore), Mandya.

Preface

The basic objective of tax reform in any country should be to establish a tax system that is economically efficient, distributionally attractive, and simple to administer.

GST is India's most ambitious indirect tax reform plan. Its objective is to levy a single national uniform tax across India on all goods and services. GST, as and when implemented, would replace a number of Central and State taxes, make India more of a national integrated market, and bring more producers into the tax net. By improving efficiency as well as revenues, it can add substantially to growth as well as helping government finances.

The current structure of taxes on goods and services in India is highly complex, highly leaky (riddled with exemptions), and characterized by a complicated rate structure.

In relation to goods, the Centre has a very complex tax structure, more complex than that of most of the States. It encompasses customs, central excise/Central value added tax (CENVAT), cesses, countervailing and special additional duties, extensive exemptions, and a multiplicity of ad valorem and specific rates. The introduction of the service tax in 1994 has been a mixed blessing. While it has broadened the tax base, its structure is complex. There is no standardized nomenclature for services, such as the harmonised system nomenclature (HSN) for goods.

The replacement of the State sales taxes by the value added tax (VAT) in 2005 marked a significant step forward in the reform of domestic trade taxes in India. Implemented by the Empowered Committee of State Finance Ministers (Chairman: Asim Dasgupta), it addressed the distortions and complexities associated with the levy of tax at the first point of sale under the erstwhile system and resulted in a major simplification of the rate structure and broadening of the tax base. Still, there are complexities under the State VAT which relate primarily to classification of goods to different tax rate schedules.

GST is a destination based comprehensive tax levy on manufacture, sale and consumption of goods and services at a national level. The introduction of GST would be a significant step in the field of indirect tax reforms in India. By subsuming a large number of Central and State taxes into a single tax, it would mitigate cascading or double taxation in a major way and pave way for a common national market. GST is a single tax on the supply of goods and services, right from the manufacturer to the consumer. Credits of input taxes paid at each stage will be available in the subsequent stage of value addition, which makes GST essentially a tax only on value addition at each stage. The final consumer will thus bear only the GST charged by the last dealer in the supply chain, with set-off benefits at all the previous stages. It will improve the ease of doing business as companies will not have to go through the hassle of paying multiple taxes and the seamless access to markets across Indian states will facilitate more efficient production and distribution systems. Implication of tax norms can help in improving tax compliance and increasing tax revenues. It can bring more transparency and better compliance. GST's implementation will improve India's image internationally and be welcomed by investors, rating agencies and multilateral institutions. GST is clearly a long-term strategy; it is expected to lead a higher growth, output, more employment opportunities, and economic inclusion.

While GST seems to be our savior, the devil exists in the details. The structural and administrative challenges involved in the implementation of GST have delayed its entry into our country. The revenue sharing model between the Centre and the States will definitely lead to a financial loss for some of the manufacturing States. Consequently, the tax rates under GST cannot be kept low, as it will impact finances of the Centre and the States. This is likely to have an inflationary impact, as it will push up the prices of many items. This will impact the entire population, as indirect taxes by nature are not equitable and are levied irrespective of your income bracket—which may be politically suicidal for any government. The tax rate under GST may be anywhere between 18 percent and 27 percent. This value is very high, considering that the global average GST/VAT rate is 16.4 percent and the average rate in Asia-Pacific is 9.88 percent and Canada and Nigeria it is just at 5 percent.

Some also have the view that, in order to appease the States, the final GST model that will be implemented is expected to be weak and far from perfect. For example, several goods have been excluded from the purview of GST like petroleum products, alcohol and electricity. The 1 percent additional tax on inter-State sales was proposed as the manufacturing States contended that they, having spent money on putting up of infrastructure, would lose out on revenue, as GST is essentially a destination tax. India is a federal nation and financial federalism is a core element of its set up. The success of this Bill lies in the proper division of powers between the Centre and the States.

Lok Sabha passed the 122nd Constitutional Amendment—Goods and Services Tax Bill on May 6, 2015. Rajya Sabha passed the 122nd Constitutional Amendment Bill with 9 amendments on August 3, 2016. Lok Sabha passed the modified 122nd Constitution Amendment Bill on August 8, 2016 approving all the 9 amendments by the Rajya Sabha.

The Bill now requires clearance of at least half (15 out of the 29) of the States to be given the President's approval. And then both the Centre and States have to pass Central GST and State GST Bills respectively and rules have to be made under them. Currently, the hope is that GST will be implemented from April 1, 2017.

This is a reviewed edited book of selected articles presented at the National Conference, sponsored by the University Grants Commission (UGC) on the topic of, "Goods and Services Tax: Impact on the Indian Economy" organized by the Economics Department of Motilal Nehru College (Evening), University of Delhi. All the articles have been reviewed and the contributors have been asked to do the changes suggested by the reviewers. As such, this edited volume is a post conference publication and hence, it does not constitute a conference proceeding.

The present volume contains 19 research articles (divided into 5 sub-themes or parts) authored by experts in the field of fiscal policy that provide deep insights into various aspects of goods and services tax (GST).

I place on record my deep sense of gratitude to all the scholars for their worthy contributions to this volume. Their views on GST would surely add, constructively, to the raging debate in the country on the implications of GST.

I take this opportunity to express my deep regards and appreciation for Dr. S.K. Sharma, Acting Principal, Motilal Nehru College (Evening), University of Delhi for his support, co-operation and advice at various stages of the completion of this work. Thanks are also due to Mr. Khemchand Jagirdar, Chairperson of the Governing Body of the college, for his moral support and encouragement. I express my gratitude to Professor K.V. Bhanu Murthy for writing the Foreword to this volume.

Finally, I thank my colleagues in the college, my students, family members, and New Century Publications, New Delhi for all the co-operation and support extended by them.

New Delhi **Anjali Agarwal**
August 2016

Major Milestones in the Journey of GST

Date/Month/Year	Event
2003	Vijay Kelkar Task Force on Indirect Taxes suggested a comprehensive Goods and Services Tax (GST) based on VAT principle.
February 28, 2006	Finance Minister Shri P. Chidambaran in his Budget Speech for the year 2006-07 mooted a proposal to introduce a National Level Goods and Services Tax (GST) by April 1, 2010.
...	Since the proposal involved reform/restructuring of not only indirect taxes levied by the Centre but also the States, the responsibility of preparing a Design and Road Map for the implementation of GST was assigned to the Empowered Committee (EC) of State Finance Ministers.
September 2009	In order to take the GST-related work further, a Joint Working Group consisting of officers from Central as well as State Government was constituted.
November 2009	Based on inputs from Government of India and States, EC released its First Discussion Paper on Goods and Services Tax in India.
March 2011	In order to amend the Constitution to enable introduction of GST, the Constitution (115th Amendment) Bill was introduced in the Lok Sabha. As per the prescribed procedure, the Bill was referred to the Standing Committee on Finance of the Parliament for examination and report.
November 8,	In pursuance of the decision taken in a

2012	meeting between the Union Finance Minister and the Empowered Committee of State Finance Ministers, a Committee on GST Design, consisting of the officials of the Government of India, State Governments and the Empowered Committee was constituted.
January 2013	The Committee on GST Design submitted its report which included the Constitution (115th) Amendment Bill.
August 2013	Parliamentary Standing Committee submitted its Report to the Lok Sabha. The recommendations of the Empowered Committee (EC) and the recommendations of the Parliamentary Standing Committee were examined in the Ministry of Finance in consultation with the Legislative Department. Most of the recommendations made by the Empowered Committee and the Parliamentary Standing Committee were accepted and the draft Amendment Bill was suitably revised.
September 2013	The final draft Constitutional Amendment Bill incorporating the above stated changes was sent to the Empowered Committee (EC) for consideration.
November 2013	EC once again made certain recommendations on the Bill after its meeting in Shillong.
March 2014	Certain recommendations of the EC were incorporated in the draft Constitution (115th Amendment) Bill. The revised draft was sent for consideration of the EC.
March 2011	The 115th Constitutional (Amendment) Bill, 2011, for the introduction of GST introduced in the Lok Sabha. It lapsed with

	the dissolution of the 15th Lok Sabha.
June 2014	The draft Constitution Amendment Bill was sent to the Empowered Committee (EC) after approval of the new Government.
December 17, 2014	Based on a broad consensus reached with EC on the contours of the Bill, the Cabinet approved the proposal for introduction of a Bill in the Parliament for amending the Constitution of India to facilitate the introduction of GST in the country.
December 19, 2014	The Bill was introduced in the Lok Sabha.
May 6, 2015	The Bill was passed by the Lok Sabha. It was then referred to the Select Committee of Rajya Sabha.
July 22, 2015	The Select Committee of Rajya Sabha submitted its report.
August 3, 2016.	Rajya Sabha passed the 122nd Constitutional Amendment Bill with 9 amendments.
August 8, 2016	Lok Sabha passed the modified 122nd Constitution Amendment Bill approving all the 9 amendments by the Rajya Sabha.
April 1, 2017	Target date for the launch of GST.

Part I:
GST: The Awaited Tax Reform

1

Will India's Proposed GST Work?

Sacchidananda Mukherjee

India is moving towards introducing goods and services tax (GST). The GST would be a multi-stage comprehensive value added tax (VAT) encompassing both goods and services. Given the federal structure of India and the fact that taxation powers have been constitutionally assigned to different governments, the introduction of GST would be a major indirect tax reform, as both the Centre (the Union Government) and State Governments will get rights to tax goods as well services at every stage of value addition in production and distribution.

The indirect tax system in India has gone through several reforms in the last two decades (Rao and Rao, 2005). At the Central level, introduction of central value added tax (CENVAT) in 2000-01 and service tax in 1994 were the major reforms. Following the recommendations of the Tax Reforms Committee, CENVAT was introduced in India which gradually unified tax rates on manufacturing and gave greater importance on account-based administration in addition to allowing for input tax credit against inputs and capital goods up to the manufacturing stage.

The Central Government introduced service tax in 1994 with an initial tax on three services. [1] Gradually, the number of services under service tax was expanded, combined with rationalization of tax rates (Rao and Chakraborty, 2013). In 2004, the input tax credit scheme for CENVAT and service tax was merged to permit cross flow of credit across these taxes. In the Union Budget 2012-13, the concept of a "negative list" for taxation of services was introduced with a list of 17 services excluded (as in 2013-14). Introduction of negative list based taxation of services resulted in transition from selective list-based taxation of services to a comprehensive approach where all services, except those in the negative list, were brought under the service tax. However, a number of services which are in the negative list are either taxed by the State Governments (e.g., service of transportation of passengers, services by way of transportation of goods, betting/gambling or lottery, access to a road or a bridge on payment of toll charges, trading of goods etc.) or by the Central government by other taxes (e.g. processes amounting to manufacture or production of goods).

Since 1999, there has been a considerable effort to bring about harmonization in the rates of taxes across states. However, there are some commodities where individual states have chosen non-standard rates of tax. There was tax competition among States (Rao and Vaillancourt, 1994) and disharmony in tax rates, number of tax schedules and exempted items (Aggarwal, 1995). The introduction of VAT replaced the sales tax system which encompassed sale of goods up to the retail stage. VAT is levied on intra-State sale of goods and input tax credit on inputs and capital goods is available only for intra-State purchases of these goods. VAT credits are adjusted against VAT and/or CST liabilities.

The introduction of VAT system in both Central and State indirect taxation resulted in the first round of cleaning up of hidden indirect taxes. [2] It is envisaged that the proposed GST will further clean up the indirect tax system by reducing cascading of taxes [3] and facilitating a nation-wide market for goods and services. Under GST, it is expected that harmonization of indirect tax structure (tax rules and regulations and tax base across States), concurrent taxation power of Centre and States at every stage of production and distribution of goods and services and joint monitoring of same taxpayers would result in better tax compliance, reduced leakage of revenue and better tax coordination between Central and State tax administrations.

The reduction of cascading of taxes and transaction costs

associated with inter-State sales of goods could facilitate higher economic growth by attracting investment. It is the expectation of the Central Government that introduction of GST will improve India's ranking in World Bank's ease of doing business as it will remove cascading of taxes as well as transaction costs involved in distribution of goods and provide services across States. [4]

In the present indirect taxation system, some sectors are taxed more than others. For example, manufacturing is taxed by both Centre and State Governments whereas services are taxed once. Some states tax agricultural products and that also selectively. Therefore, the present indirect taxation system not only provides unequal tax base between the Centre and State governments but also distorts the consumer choice by differential taxation of goods and services.

The objective of this paper is to provide a brief overview of the present system of taxation of goods and services. It would be followed by an introduction of the proposed goods and services tax (GST) system. In the last section, we will explore the possible impacts of GST on Indian economy.

Taxation of Goods

There are four major taxes on domestically produced goods in India. First, CENVAT is a value added tax levied and collected by the Central Government on the manufacture of goods. CENVAT is often described as a first point sales tax, as beyond this point, taxation power of goods rests on State governments. CENVAT is uniform across States and input tax credits (CENVAT Credit) are allowed against Central excise duty, service tax (since 2004), as well as countervailing duty (CVD) and "cesses" thereof (for imported goods/inputs) (since the era of MODVAT). Input tax credits are allowed against purchase of inputs as well as capital goods. Among the other three taxes, State sales tax or VAT and entry tax (in lieu of Octroi) are levied, collected and retained by the State Governments. The Central sales tax (CST) is levied by the

Central Government on inter-State sales of goods but it is collected and retained by the exporting (origin) States.

The rates of State taxes vary across States as do the rules and regulations. For example, present standard VAT rate varies from 12.5 percent for a majority of States to 14.5 percent (e.g. in Assam, West Bengal and Rajasthan). For goods which are under State VAT, input tax credits against intra-State purchases are allowed. For the majority of States, entry tax (in lieu of Octroi) is commodity specific (e.g., Bihar, Himachal Pradesh, Gujarat) and some States do not allow an input tax credit against entry tax (e.g., Assam, Karnataka, Odisha). Entry tax rates vary across States and commodities. CST is levied on inter-State sales. It is expected that under the GST regime, the tax structure across States will be harmonized and multiple taxes will be subsumed under the GST. The present system results in substantial transaction costs for businesses, as they have to comply with different State tax rules and regulations with different tax rates for same commodity, and it discourages voluntary compliance which leads to revenue leakage.

The present system of taxation of goods can best be described as an origin-based tax system where the manufacturing (origin or exporting) State collects CST on goods being sold inter-State. Since it is a tax collected by the origin State, the destination (importing) State does not allow input tax credit against CST. Therefore, CST remains a stranded cost for inter-State dealers and manufacturers using goods procured from other States. Though input tax credit against CST sales is allowed, withholding of input tax credits for various reasons is common in many States (e.g., in case of consignment/branch transfers). The present rate of CST is 2 percent (maximum limit) at which States could levy entry tax. Many States, mostly special category States, do not levy CST. However, if the goods are sold from the origin State to the final consumer (B2C transactions), the origin State levies CST at the rate equivalent to State VAT whereas the destination State does not get any tax on the transaction.

However, if the incoming good is imported for trading (B2B transactions), the import attracts full State VAT in addition to entry tax depending on the type of good and State of operation. In States where entry tax is collected on behalf of local governments and the revenue is passed on to them, entry tax remains a stranded cost for these States (e.g., Karnataka, Odisha) as no input tax credit against entry tax is allowed. A few States provide input tax credits against entry tax provided the goods are meant for further value addition or trade in the State concerned (e.g., Bihar, Gujarat).

The present system of tax on inter-state movement of goods provides an option to manufacturers to either locate their branch offices and/or set up their own distribution networks across all the States of their operations so that they could send the goods as branch/consignment transfers and avoid paying CST and entry tax. Often the cost of establishing branch offices or own distribution networks constraints businesses to scale up and encourage inefficiency in production as well as distribution of goods or providing services.

Therefore, the present system is not conducive for evolving a seamless common market for goods and services. In addition, businesses face different tax rules and regulations in each state. Since legal trade attracts multiple taxes, the system also encourages illegal trade at least of high value goods (e.g. tobacco products, alcohol). Therefore, the removal of CST and entry tax from inter-State movements of goods will help to shift indirect taxation system from origin-based to destination-based, which is a desired outcome of the proposed GST regime. At present, consumers in importing States pay taxes to exporting States where manufacturing is taking place. Since the manufacturing base in India is not evenly distributed across States, a few States gain from this distortionary tax system.

Depending on the definitions of goods and services, and the stage of value addition (production or distribution), the Constitution of India assigns taxation power to Centre as well as State Governments. The CENVAT is levied on manufactured goods at the factory gate whereas manufacturers also attract State VAT on sale of the goods. Since manufacturers are assessed on State VAT, input tax credits are allowed on purchases of inputs (including capital goods) within the State, adjusted against VAT and/or CST payable to State Government.

Similarly, manufacturers adjust input taxes paid on input goods (CENVAT and/or CVD), plants and machinery, and services (service tax) against tax payable to Central Government. Since traders (distributors) are not liable to tax under CENVAT, taxes paid by manufacturers (Central excise duty) remain a stranded cost for traders. The service taxes paid on input services by traders are not adjusted against their tax liability to State Government. Similarly, service providers are not liable to State VAT. Hence, any VAT paid on input goods remains a stranded cost for them.

The non-allowance of input tax credits breaks the chain, leading to cascading which is not conducive for businesses as it causes substantial locking up of working capital as unpaid credits. The system also does not provide enough incentives to businesses to take registration. Non-inclusion of a large section of businesses under the tax net is not conducive for the economy as well as the taxation system. These features of the present indirect taxation system encourage a large part of economic activities to evade taxes and generate unaccounted income (NIPFP, 2014). For the tax department, non-participation by a segment of the economy can induce lower confidence in the tax regime resulting in higher non-compliance even among segments which would normally pay taxes. In addition, input taxes are adjusted only against tax payable to output whereas duties, surcharges and cesses paid on input goods and services remain as stranded costs for an assessee.

Taxation of Services

Service tax is a Central tax levied by the Central Government on all services except a few services which are exempted (e.g., education, medical and health services) by keeping them under the negative list in the Union Budget 2012-13. Since these are not zero rated, the exempted services cannot claim refund of CENVAT paid on purchase of goods, tax paid on services and those remain as stranded costs for them. Central government allows selective cross credits across CENVAT and service tax provided the assessee falls either under the Central excise and/or service tax assessment. State governments also levy stand-alone taxes on a few services (e.g., passenger and goods tax, luxury tax on hotels and lodging houses, entertainment and advertisement tax) but do not allow input tax credits against their VAT purchases. In addition, being assessee of Central Government, service providers cannot claim ITC against VAT purchases of goods.

Proposed GST

The key features of the proposed new GST regime are briefly summarized as follows:

1. The tax is to cover all goods and services; it is however, proposed that there would be a small negative list of goods and services which will not be taxed under the GST. All other supplies of goods and services would be subject to tax.
2. Dual GST: there will be two taxes levied on each supply—one as a part of the Central GST and the other as a part of the State GST.
3. It is proposed that the GST regime would have two rates of tax, a lower rate for supply of specially identified goods and services and the rest of the supplies would be taxable at a standard rate. [5]

- Some supplies that are to remain outside the base for GST are petrol, diesel, ATF, crude petroleum, natural gas, alcoholic beverages for human consumption, real estate and electricity.
- The constitutional amendment allows for the incorporation of petrol, diesel, ATF, natural gas and crude petroleum in the base at a subsequent date.

4. On inter-state supplies, it is proposed that the Centre will levy and collect Integrated GST (IGST)—the importing

dealer can claim input tax credit for IGST paid on these goods against taxes payable on subsequent transactions. While in principle, all governments are in agreement that Central Sales Tax regime would be removed when GST is introduced, this tax would remain on goods and services which are explicitly excluded from the GST regime.

5. It is proposed that for the standard rate, there would be a band which allows the states some flexibility in fixing rates.
6. In order to protect the states from any loss of revenue in the process of reform, Central government has proposed to compensate for any loss of revenue for first five years of introduction of GST.
7. So as to put in place a mechanism which ensures the creation and sustenance of GST which is comprehensive and comparable across States, all policy decisions regarding GST are to be taken on the advice of the GST Council where the Central government is to have a 33.33 percent vote with the rest being assigned to the states.
8. GST is to be administered separately by the Central and State tax administrations. It is proposed that there would be common registration and common portal for filing of returns. There are no clear decisions available in the public domain on whether there would be further coordination between the two sets of tax administrations.
9. In the GST regime, exports will be zero rated and imports will attract GST in addition to basic customs duty.

In the proposed system of GST, both Central and State Government will have concurrent taxation power of goods and services at all stages of value addition (production and distribution or trade). The proposed system is an improvement over the present system. It will reduce the cascading of taxes arising due to non-allowance of input tax credits for input goods (or services) for production/distribution of services (or goods) due to inter-jurisdiction (cross tax authority) nature of taxes, as well as differences of a non-overlapping nature in taxation power of goods and services. Second, it will reduce cascading from non-allowance of input tax credits against inter-State sales. However, inconvenience arising due to non-allowance of inter-jurisdiction (cross tax authority) input tax credits may not arise, even though under the proposed GST regime, inter-jurisdiction ITC flow is not allowed.

Under the proposed system, there will be parallel tax payment and credit systems—one for Central GST (CGST) and another one for State GST (SGST), where input tax credits for each tax will be adjusted before paying taxes to respective tax authorities. Since GST is a multistage value added tax, tax liability will depend on the level of value addition. Under the proposed system, continuation of input tax credit chain is ensured even for inter-State sales. For inter-State sales, the exporting dealers will pay Integrated GST (IGST) to Central Tax Authority by adjusting input tax credits arising against SGST, CGST and IGST (if any). The IGST liability will comprise of CGST, SGST (possibly rate prevailing in destination State) and any other taxes imposed on inter-State sales of goods. Dealers in the destination State will pay CGST and SGST liabilities on subsequent sales by adjusting IGST credit pool. First, IGST will be utilized to pay CGST and then SGST.

The proposed tax system will subsume both Central and State indirect taxes and levies. On the combined tax base, a dual GST (CGST and SGST) will be levied. The details of State and Central taxes that will be subsumed under GST are presented in Table 1.1.

However, in the GST system, cascading of taxes on account of exclusions of goods from GST, exemptions, and thresholds (or any turnover based exemptions) will continue. Non-inclusion of certain fossil fuels (e.g., petrol, diesel, ATF, natural gas and crude petroleum) and electricity which are directly and indirectly used as inputs for all goods and services, will retain substantial cascading of taxes of the present system and will hamper competitiveness of domestic industries in international market (Mukherjee and Rao, 2015a).

By reducing cascading of taxes, GST would provide relief to business community as they do not have to block substantial working capital as unpaid input tax credits.

Table 1.1: Central and State Taxes to be Subsumed by GST

State Taxes	Central Taxes
-State value added tax/sales tax -Entertainment tax (other than the tax levied by the local bodies) -Central sales tax (levied by the Centre and collected by the States) -Entry tax (in lieu of octroi) -Purchase tax -Luxury tax -Taxes on lottery, betting and gambling -State cesses and surcharges (related to supply of goods and services)	-Central excise duty -Additional excise duty -Excise duty levied under the Medicinal and Toilet Preparations (Excise Duties) Act, 1955 -Service tax -Additional customs duty (commonly known as countervailing duty) -Special additional duty of customs -Central surcharges and cesses (related to supply of goods and services)

Source: Government of India (2015).

Possible Impact of GST on GDP Growth

It expected that GST will correct some of the structural rigidities of the present indirect tax system and increase economic efficiency. Reduction of cascading of taxes and transactions costs—associated with inter-state transactions—will enhance efficiency in production and distribution of goods and services. It will also expand the scope and spread of markets for businesses and encourage investment. Increase in efficiency and competition is expected to lower the prices and in the long-run attract more investment and hence enhanced growth.

However, available estimates on impact of GST on economic growth are old and not free from criticism. However, the effect of GST on Indian economy will not be instantaneous. It is to be noted that a part of the gains of removing cascading of taxes in our indirect tax system have been already reaped by introducing value added tax system for both Central and State taxes. The gains from GST will also be limited due to exclusions of major energy inputs (like electricity, diesel, natural gas) out of the GST system. However, removal of cascading of taxes in the proposed GST regime will also be substantial and it is likely that it will reduce the costs to entrepreneurs, encourage investment and increase economic growth. The major benefits of GST will come from improvement in investment climate and possible improvement in compliance due to joint monitoring of same tax payers by both Centre and State tax administrations. A rise in compliance could also be induced by encouraging invoice based transactions. Minimising cash based transactions by encouraging electronic transactions could help to rein in generation and propagation of unaccounted income.

Possible Impact of GST on Inflation

As discussed earlier, in our present system, services are not taxed as much as our manufactured goods. Possibly in the GST regime, taxes on services will increase and taxes on manufactured goods will decrease. Since the overall impact of GST is expected to be revenue neutral, if the benefits of removal of cascading of taxes and transaction costs are passed on to the consumers, the prices will fall. If the benefits are not forwarded, it will at least expand the tolerance limit of businesses to absorb the stochastic shocks in input costs—e.g. rise in fuel prices, exchange rate volatility—and not to pass on the costs to the consumers immediately.

It is also expected that the GST regime will encourage competition in the market and consumers will be better off. Since the proposed GST system is expected to be revenue neutral and does not plan for expansion of tax payers' base—by reducing the threshold for GST registration and by inclusions of exempted goods—there is no additional factor that could influence inflation expectations. International experience shows that a short-term increase in prices might be observed, due to adjustment in prices during transition, but it should settle down quickly. Governments tend to monitor prices in the transition to make sure the benefits are passed on in sectors where there are benefits.

Conclusions

One of the objectives behind introduction of VAT system was to capture information at the upstream of value chains through allowance of input tax credit. However, in the present indirect tax system, the information chain breaks down due to differences in jurisdiction of taxation and inter-state movement of goods. Inherent incentive compatible system of ITC is expected to encourage formalisation of businesses. The presence of large informal sector in India shows that the opportunity cost of being under the tax system cannot always outweigh the benefits (Mukherjee and Rao, 2015b). The presence of informal credit and labour markets, as well as a large domestic demand for locally produced goods and services, often leads to unaccounted-for incomes that avoid taxation. Since the new tax regime is expected to work through more integrated and redefined supply chains, for the regime to be beneficial and successful, it is important that more and more enterprises find it useful to be a part of the GST regime.

It is expected that the introduction of GST will remove the structural rigidities of the present indirect tax system and provide a common market for goods and services. GST would be an improvement as it would reduce cascading of taxes and transaction costs associated with inter-state sales of goods. This could facilitate achieving a seamless common market. It is also expected that seamless access to markets across Indian states will facilitate more efficient production and distribution systems. This could also minimise costs of operation and enhance economic growth by attracting investment and releasing working capital.

Joint monitoring of the same taxpayers should also result in better tax compliance, minimise revenue leakage and improve tax coordination between federal and state tax administrators.

There are several challenges if a GST is introduced, which can be classified under two broad headings: design and structural issues, and administration and institutional issues (Mukherjee, 2015). For example, on the design, the decision to exclude major fossil fuels (petrol/gasoline, diesel, ATF, natural gas and crude petroleum) and electricity from the GST will mean that there will still be substantial cascading of taxes (Mukherjee and Rao, 2015a). This will jeopardise the scope for improving the competitiveness of domestic industries in the international market.

On administration, if the GST is administered separately by the federal and state tax administrators, taxpayers who previously faced a single tax administration (for example, retailers or service providers) will instead face two tax administrations. Complying with different tax authorities for a single transaction could enhance compliance costs, which could work against voluntary compliance. One possible option could be to establish joint tax administration for many functions (Rao and Mukherjee, 2010).

A more harmonised taxation system, like a GST, restricts the freedom of individual governments to deviate from a common tax structure. Given the federal structure of India, harmonisation of tax rules and regulations is more important than harmonisation of tax rates from a business perspective.

If international experience is anything to go by, it is unlikely that a faultless GST will be designed and rolled out in India as a single event. But some structural faults could easily be addressed and rectified. Given the diversity involved in design and administration, an Indian GST will be unique. How successful it is in terms of compliance and revenue mobilisation will largely depend on the following:

1. Modernisation and simplification of tax administration.
2. Provision of incentives for tax invoice based transactions.
3. Facilitating voluntary compliance by simplifications of rules and regulations.

4. Provisions of tax payers services.
5. Tax coordination and automatic exchange of information across tax jurisdictions.

To minimise leakage of revenue, a system of cooperative tax compliance with involvement of consumers, tax payers, tax administration and tax intermediaries may be useful. Reduction in leakage of tax revenue will release the pressure from tax rate to rise with rising revenue needs and therefore will provide larger income at the hands of consumers to spend on goods and services. It will expand domestic market for goods and services and encourage investment and growth in the economy.

*This article is based on a paper (Mukherjee, 2015) originally presented at the Tax and Transfer Policy Institute at the Crawford School of Public Policy, the Australian National University on September 25, 2015.

Endnotes

1. Tax on telephone billing, tax on general insurance premium and tax on stock brokerage commission.
2. For majority of Indian States, sales tax was first point tax on sales which was not able to capture value addition in subsequent sales (Aggarwal, 1995).
3. Arising due to constitutionally assigned taxation power to Centre to tax majority of services, and to tax manufacturing of goods (first point sale tax) and several other taxes on inter-state movements of goods–CST, entry tax and local area taxes (local area development tax).
4. India's rank in World Bank's ease of doing business is 130 out of 189 countries, as on June 2015: http://www.doingbusiness.org/rankings, last accessed on November 12, 2015.
5. There is also a proposal to levy a high tax rate on luxury goods like motor vehicles (CEA Report).

References

Aggarwal, P.K. (1995), "Incidence of Major Indirect Taxes in India", NIPFP, New Delhi.

Government of India (2015), "Report of the Select Committee on the

Constitution (One Hundred and Twenty-Second Amendment) Bill, 2014", Presented to the Rajya Sabha on July 22, 2015, Rajya Sabha, Parliament of India, Government of India, New Delhi.

Mukherjee, S. (2015), "Present State of Goods and Services Tax (GST) Reform in India", Working Paper No. 06/2015, Tax and Transfer Policy Institute, Crawford School of Public Policy, Australian National University, Canberra, Australia.

Mukherjee, S. and R. Kavita Rao (2015a), "Policy Options for Including Petroleum, Natural Gas and Electricity in the Goods and Services Tax", *Economic and Political Weekly*, Vol. 50, No. 9, pp. 98-107.

Mukherjee, S. and R. Kavita Rao (2015b), "Factors Influencing Unincorporated Enterprises to Register under Value Added Tax (VAT): An Analysis with Enterprises Survey Data", Working Paper No. 145, National Institute of Public Finance and Policy (NIPFP), New Delhi.

National Institute of Public Finance and Policy (NIPFP) (2014), "Study on Unaccounted Incomes in India", Project Report Submitted to Central Board of Direct Taxes, Department of Revenue, Ministry of Finance, Government of India, New Delhi.

Rao, M. Govinda and François Vaillancourt (1994), "Interstate Tax Disharmony in India: A Comparative Perspective", *Publius*, Vol. 24, No. 4, pp. 99-114.

Rao, R. Kavita and P. Chakraborty (2013), "Revenue Implications of GST and Estimation of Revenue Neutral Rate: A State-wise Analysis", report Submitted to the Empowered Committee of State Finance Ministers, New Delhi.

Rao, R. Kavita and S. Mukherjee (2010), "Administration of GST: Can We Continue with Present Structures?", Background Paper for the Workshop on GST, NIPFP, March 2010.

Rao, M. Govinda and R. Kavita Rao (2005), "Trends and Issues in Tax Policy and Reform in India", *India Policy Forum*, Global Economy and Development Program, The Brookings Institution, Vol. 2, No. 1, pp. 55-122.

2

Value Added Tax (VAT) and GST: A Comparison

Mandeep Kaur

Introduction

The recent reforms of indirect taxation in India aim to introduce a dual goods and services tax (GST) wherein the power to levy tax on goods and services will lie both with the Centre and the States. The Central GST (CGST) will subsume a number of central government taxes that includes Central excise duty, additional excise duty, service tax, countervailing duty and special additional duty of customs among others. Sales tax or the state value added tax is a significant tax that shall be subsumed under the State GST (SGST). GST reforms have been sought after in order to do away with shortcomings of earlier commodity tax systems viz. the excise duty on production and the sales tax on consumption. Goods and service tax has been hailed to cure the Indian tax system of its complex administration besides its cascading effect and the resultant non-neutrality.

However, each of the earlier tax reforms viz. the CENVAT and the State VAT too had the above said objectives at the time when they were introduced. GST seems to be more modified version of CENVAT. This paper takes a detailed literature review of indirect tax reforms in India beginning with the introduction MODVAT in the year 1986, with the objective of making a comparative analysis of excise duty, value added tax, sales tax and GST in order to assess the benefits of GST in terms of administrative ease and neutrality.

Excise Duty

The Indian tax system was defined by large number of excise

duties at the manufacturing level before the 1986 MODVAT reform. To begin with, the tax was imposed on few goods only. Over the years, in order to meet the rising revenue requirements, the tax rates and the tax base were expanded. Rao and Rao (2006) noted that initially the tax was imposed on raw materials and intermediaries for administrative convenience (Rao and Rao, 2005-06). To meet increasing revenue requirements, final consumer goods too were brought within the ambit of union excise duties, and by the year 1975-76, all manufactured goods were taxed.

The system of Union excise duties was unable to meet the rising revenue requirements of the Central Government. The share of Union excise duties in the total tax revenue had increased from about 46 percent in 1960-61 to 51 percent in 1976-77. Since then, the falling share of Union excise duties has been widely documented. It had declined to 43 percent in 1990-91 and there has been a corresponding increase in customs duty, mainly on account of rising customs tariff rate (Aggarwal, 1991). The falling growth rate of excise duty revenue has been well documented during the period before the 1990s (Narayana and Gupta, March 1990). A large number of factors were identified for such state of affairs.

Firstly, the specific nature of excise duty has been a major source of falling tax buoyancy from excise duty (Jha, 1977). The report states that the revenue growth from excise duty was lower than sales tax on account of excise duty rates being specific while sales tax was ad valorem. Thus, it has been stated that even though there was a rise in union excise duty tax rates, the conversion of most excise duties into specific tax during the period 1975-86 led to falling revenue growth from excise duties (Narayana and Gupta, 1990).

The tax at the first point of sale or on manufacturing had problems relating to defining manufacturing, determining assessable manufacturing value and concentration of tax burden at one stage. All these led to increasing disputes in claiming excise revenue and increasing uncertainty with regard to tax revenue collection (Bagchi, 1994). Hence, not only the tax base of union excise duties on manufactured goods without the trading margins was very narrow, the revenue from excise duties was uncertain too. Also with no exclusive provision of service tax, a large component of manufacturing value was presented as *post-manufacturing services* in order to bypass the excise duty obligations.

Hence, in order to meet the rising revenue requirements, inputs and capital goods were also brought under the ambit of union excise duties. This had led to cascading i.e. rise in the prices of goods by more than the element of tax in it. Multilevel taxation—say excise on input and excise on manufacturing or between different taxes like excise on input and sales tax on manufacturing without *adequate* set off for inputs, leads to substantial input taxation. This led to significant production and consumption distortion (Agarwal, 1995).

Within the States, the sales tax has been a major source of revenue. The share of sales tax till the year 1995 remained more or less at 60 percent. Theoretically, sales tax can be levied at one or more stages in the process of production and distribution of goods. These levels could be manufacturing, wholesale and retail.

However, most states levied sales tax at the first point of sale. Sales tax has received severe criticism from economic point of view not only for their cascading and the resulting economic distortions on production and consumption, but also for its uncontrolled incidence.

For administrative ease, the base of excise and sales tax has overlapped and about 3/4th of sales tax revenue is collected at the first point of sale that is manufacturing (Narayana and Gupta, 1990). R.J. Chelliah (Chelliah, 1980) notes that despite the constitutional provision of non-overlapping of tax base for central government and state government for the purpose of excise and sales duty, in practice and for administrative convenience, both the bases have overlapped. The scope of excise duty at the time when it was conceived was very limited. However, the extension of excise to 'all manufactured goods in factory sector not elsewhere specified' led to significant overlapping.

On the other hand, most of the states levied single point sales tax at manufacturing level. However, the scope of multi-stage sales tax extends to value added at wholesale and retail level. Hence, the sales tax was levied on a price inclusive of excise and excise was collected on sales tax paid in earlier stages. This has led to manufacturing getting taxed by two independent tax systems, producing significant cascading and price distortions. The duty drawback scheme that was extended to excise duty has not been made available to sales tax for administrative difficulty.

It can thus, be concluded that Constitutional provision of allocating excise duty to the Centre and sales tax to the States was also one of the fundamental reasons for tax cascading. While on the one hand, tax base of sales tax is large, its administration at multistage level is difficult. On the other hand, while the base of excise is small, it has significant negative implications for revenue to the Central government. In order to enlarge the tax base, larger number of goods was brought into the tax net. These also came under the ambit of sales tax due to their administrative ease. Hence, multilevel taxing led to cascading.

Another aspect of sales tax regime that came under criticism in a federal entity like India was the lack of harmony among States' sales tax rates. Unhealthy competition among States with respect to sales tax rates led to 'rate war' among States that led to adverse effects on revenue growth (First Discussion Paper on Goods and Service Tax in India, 2009).

It, thus, seems that there was strict urgency of a tax system that provided for input tax credit in order to do away with cascading and its resultant economic distortions that the Union excise duties had brought in its process of evolution.

MODVAT

Under the MODVAT scheme, the scope of goods claiming input tax credit was enlarged. All commodities, except textiles, petroleum and its products, tobacco and its products and plant and machinery were covered under the scheme. Under the scheme, tax credit can be availed against Union excise duty or countervailing duty paid on inputs *against tax liability on output.* It was only in 1994-95 that capital goods, petroleum products and specified spun yarns were covered under MODVAT. Also, small-scale industrial enterprises could opt to pay normal excise duty instead of concessional duty in order to avail MODVAT input credit facility. Later, the condition of matching raw materials/capital with output for availing MODVAT input credit was withdrawn which facilitated manufacturers to access MODVAT input credit facility in order to pay for their excise tax liability.

During the 1990s, most of rates have been converted from specific to ad valorem and the MODVAT rates have been reduced and exemptions have been withdrawn. By the year 1991, there were nine rate categories, with rates varying from 1 to 8 percent for necessities to 225 percent for luxury items (Aggarwal, "Modified Value Added Tax (MODVAT): Structure and Resource Mobilisation", 1996).

Hence, MODVAT was applied to free the tax system of its complexity, uncontrolled incidence, and small tax base applicable to first point of sale, cascading effects and production inefficiency.

The MODVAT scheme of commodity taxation has been stated to be different from the general value added taxation for a number of reasons.

Firstly, as observed by Purohit (Purohit, M.C., 1993) the MODVAT scheme had large number of exemptions and concessional taxation of goods produced by small-scale manufacturers and because of the system of notional and deemed tax credits allowed to some manufacturers. The scheme of notional tax credit provided for tax credit to medium and large industries when inputs were purchased from small-scale manufacturers and for which no excise was paid or paid at a concessional rate.

Under the deemed tax credit scheme, MODVAT credit could be availed at certain rates for certain inputs without production of relevant documents. It was introduced with the objective of incentivizing small manufacturers.

Exemptions alter the effective rate of tax, thereby introducing multiplicity of effective tax rates. The general VAT principles call for at most 3 rates of taxation. Besides, exemptions also introduce gaps in the tax credit chain causing significant cascading. Purchases from exempt sellers cannot be claimed for the purpose of input tax credit for the tax paid by these sellers on their purchases and which remains a part of seller's price.

Secondly, the limited coverage of MODVAT scheme, could nullify the cascading effect to a very limited extent. The share of sales tax exceeded 30 percent of effective tax rate for many commodities. Despite the set off facility provided under MODVAT, excise duty's contribution varied from 20 to 40 percent (Agarwal, 1995).

Thirdly, during the 1990s, revenue from MODVAT fell down on account of rising MODVAT credit and falling gross revenue from Union excise duties. Gross revenue from excise duty fell down on account of falling tax rate and rising share of exports in manufacturing (which are exempt from excise duty). The extension of MODVAT input credit scheme to larger number of goods, including raw material and capital goods and measures taken to facilitate the use of MODVAT input credit scheme led to rising share of MODVAT credit. However, falling excise and customs duty rates and the restriction on using input credit facility for capital goods only after the capital good has been put to use tended to reduce the MODVAT credit. The overall trend has been of falling net revenue (as percentage of GDP) over the period 1986-87 to 1995-96.

Fourthly, there have been large number of MODVAT rates which is not preferable to a single VAT rate that reduces disputes in commodity classification. Also, higher the number of rates, larger is the compliance cost and cost of administration.

CenVAT and State VAT

The Budget of 2000-01 replaced MODVAT by CenVAT. It allowed for credit of excise duty, special excise duty, additional duties of excise and countervailing duties paid on inputs and capital goods for the purpose of manufacturing of goods on which duty has to be paid. This credit was to be used to pay excise duty on final product. Manufacturers of duty exempt goods were not allowed to claim input credit (Purohit, M.C., 1993).

Under CenVAT, the rate was reduced to a general rate of 16 percent, besides the special excise of 8 or 16 percent. The number of effective rates, however may have been more than these with the large number of exemptions. However, exemptions notifications were reduced over the years. Besides, the process of converting specific rates into ad valorem rates continued with the objective of increasing revenue from excise duties.

From the revenue point of view, the revenue growth from excise duty has never been high. But revenue growth from service tax and excise duty combined together has been significant, as a result of the reform measures taken (First Discussion Paper on Goods and Service Tax in India, 2009).

The CenVAT suffered from the same shortcomings as did MODVAT—its structure did not reflect the exact principles of general VAT as practised in other countries on account of exemptions, concessions, the reintroduction of deemed credit scheme (which was withdrawn in the budget of 2003-04) in textile industry.

The shortcomings of sales tax led to trade and industry lobby for complete abolition of sales tax. These demands became more vociferous with the coming of CenVAT, when no credit was provided for excise duty or service tax paid by traders for sales tax paid by them. Efforts were made to replace sales tax with State VAT which culminated in the Conference of Chief Ministers and Finance Ministers held on November 19, 1999 to ratify the replacement. The state of Haryana was the first one to replace its sales tax with state VAT during the year 2003 (Purohit, M.C., 1993).

It follows a three rate structure of 1 percent (applicable to jewellery), 4 percent (applicable to inputs and some basic necessities goods) and a standard rate of 12.5 percent (applicable to residual goods). All the rates are termed as *uniform floor rate*. Refund can be claimed under the State VAT when the commodity used is an input (Chakraborty and Datta, 2004). Also, a set off in State VAT is given not only on inputs but also on earlier purchases (First Discussion Paper on Goods and Service Tax in India, 2009).

Need for Goods and Services Tax

Despite the efforts at expanding tax base for Central Government, without the simultaneous cascading effects of taxation through the introduction of Central VAT and State VAT, the fact remain that CenVAT is essentially a tax on manufacturing which itself is a narrow base. Services have been brought under the ambit of Union taxation and service tax can be claimed for the purpose of input tax credit. However, states still cannot levy tax on services. Tax cascading still remains significant on account of large number of exemptions in both CenVAT and State VAT. Further, tax credit on state taxes paid in one State cannot be availed in another State. The existence of Central sales tax on inter-State sales, imposed by Central government but collected by the origin State is another cause of tax cascading as no credit is allowed for Central sales tax by any level of government (Poddar and Ahmad, 2009).

The Constitution (122nd Amendment) Bill that has been passed by the Rajya Sabha seeks to alter the scheme of fiscal powers distribution as envisaged in the Constitution. The dual GST as proposed by the Bill taxes the same taxable event, i.e. supply of goods and services, simultaneously by both the Centre and the States. Hence, both Centre and States have been empowered to impose GST across the value chain from the stage of manufacturing to the stage of consumption, with the credit of GST to be used for dispensing the GST liability on output, thereby avoiding tax on tax. This scheme will also ensure that the tax base gets broadened (First Discussion Paper on Goods and Service Tax in India, 2009).

The following are the salient features of the proposed GST reform:

Dual GST: Centre would levy and collect Central Goods and Services Tax (CGST), and States would levy and collect the State Goods and Services Tax (SGST) on all transactions within a State. The input tax credit of CGST would be used for discharging the CGST liability on the output at each stage. Similarly, the credit of SGST paid on inputs would be used for paying the SGST on output. No cross utilization of credit is permitted.

Integrated Goods and Services Tax (IGST) on all inter-State supply of goods and services will be levied by the Central Government. The IGST mechanism has been developed to achieve the objective of seamless input tax credit chain across states on inter-State transactions (First Discussion Paper on Goods and Service Tax in India, 2009). The IGST will be paid by the inter-State seller on the sale of goods to the Central Government after the credit of IGST, CGST and SGST on purchases is adjusted. The credit of IGST will be claimed by the importing dealer when output tax liability of CGST and SGST is discharged in own State.

GST rates are expected to be uniform across the country, with tax band over the floor rates of CGST, SGST and IGST. The threshold exemption is common for both CGST and SGST, with output of taxpayers below the threshold exempt from payment of GST. The exempt goods and services have been kept to the minimum.

The First Discussion Paper on Goods and Services Tax in India (2009) points out the precise aspects of the current VAT regime that the GST reform seeks to achieve. Firstly, the CenVAT still does not include large number of central taxes and for a large number of taxes, the input tax credit cannot be availed. Secondly, the CenVAT fails to capture value addition below the manufacturing level. Hence, the tax base of mere manufacturing is small from revenue growth point of view. Thirdly, the state level VAT does not include large number of State level taxes for the purpose of input tax credit. Fourthly, the State VAT does not provide for set off for CenVAT paid at earlier stages of production. Fifthly, the State VAT does not provide for set off for service tax paid on earlier stages of production.

The proposed GST reform, seeks to address the above shortcomings of the current CenVAT and State level VAT. Firstly, the reform will have wider coverage of taxes, including service tax, for the purpose of set off. The Central sales tax will get phased out over the years, to be replaced by IGST. Secondly, the GST reform seeks to expand the tax base for both the Central and State governments.

Every transaction of goods and services would simultaneously get taxed by CGST and SGST, except the exempt goods and services and those below the threshold limit. Both the taxes will be imposed on the same price of the commodity, unlike the current State VAT system, which imposes tax on commodity price inclusive of CenVAT.

Conclusion

The proposed goods and services tax is the next logical step to reformation of Indian indirect tax system. The CenVAT along with service taxes have already achieved significant broadening of tax base. The introduction of State VAT has introduced ITC on State sales tax. However, tax cascading remains significant in the case on inter-State sales and numerous exemptions. The proposed GST streamlines the current tax scheme by bringing the same base under the ambit of both CGST and SGST with the simultaneous set off for tax paid on inputs to their respective governments. Besides, the design of IGST meets the long pending demand of traders' lobby to create an integrated market.

References

Agarwal, P.K., (1995), "Incidence of Major Indirect Taxes in India", NIPFP, New Delhi.

Aggarwal, P.K. (1991), "Composition and Growth of Major Union Taxes", NIPFP, New Delhi.

Aggarwal, P.K. (1996), "Modified Value Added Tax (MODVAT): Structure and Resource Mobilisation", NIPFP, New Delhi.

Bagchi, A. (1994), "Reform of Domestic Trade Taxes in India: Issues and Options", NIPFP, New Delhi.

Chakraborty, P. and U. Datta (2004), "Revenue Implications of Introducing Value Added Tax at State Level", NIPFP, New Delhi.

First Discussion Paper on Goods and Service Tax in India, November, 2009, Empowered Committee of State Finance Ministers, New Delhi.

Jha Committee (1977), "Report of Indirect Taxation Inquiry Committee", Part 1, Ministry of Finance, Government of India.

Narayana, A. and R. Gupta (1990), "A Comparative Growth Study of Central Excise and Sales Tax Revenues", Report submitted to Central Board of Excise and Customs, Ministry of Finance, Government of India, NIPFP, New Delhi.

Poddar, S. and E. Ahmad (2009), "Goods and Service Tax Reforms and Intergovernmental Considerations", Working Paper No. 1/2009, Department of Economic Affairs, Ministry of Finance, Government of India.

Purohit, M.C. (1993), "Adoption of Value Added Tax in India: Problems and Prospects", *Economic and Political Weekly*, March 6.

Purohit, M.C. (1993), "Value Added Tax: Experiences of India and Other Countries", Gayatri Publications, New Delhi.

Rao, M.G. and R.K. Rao (2005-06), "Trends and Issues in Tax Policy and Reform in India", in Suman Berry, B. Bosworth and A. Panagriya, 'India Economic Forum', New Delhi: Sage Publications, pp. 55-107.

3

Impact of Goods and Services Tax

Vibha Gupta

GST (goods and services tax) would be a single uniform national tax levied across India on all the goods and services. In GST, all indirect taxes including excise duty, octroi, central sales tax (CST) and value added tax (VAT) will be subsumed under a single regime. It will be a significant step towards a comprehensive indirect tax reform as it is expected to bring efficiency and transparency in the indirect tax mechanism in India. Further, it will encourage an unbiased tax structure that is neutral to business processes and geographical locations. Given the enormity of the implication of GST, it requires a consensus among all political parties and States.

The goods and services tax (GST) is aimed at creating a single, unified market that will benefit both corporates and the economy. The changed indirect tax system GST (goods and service tax) is planned to be executed in India shortly. Several countries have implemented this tax system starting with France—the first country to introduce GST. Goods and service tax is a new story of VAT which gives a widespread setoff for input tax credit and subsuming many indirect taxes from state and national level. The GST implementation is not yet declared by the Government and the drafting of GST law is still under process and a clear picture will be available only after the announcement of its implementation. An Article has been drafted, encompassing the introduction which covers the meaning of tax, the traditional tax system, followed by meaning and key features of GST. It has also tried to highlight the objectives and benefits of the proposed GST.

Introduction

The word tax is derived from the Latin word 'taxare', meaning to estimate. A tax is not a voluntary payment or donation, but an enforced contribution, obtained pursuant to the legislative authority and is any contribution imposed by government whether under the name of toll, tribute, impost, duty, custom, excise, subsidy, aid, supply, or any other name.

Tax policies play an important role in the economy through their impact on both efficiency and equity. A good tax system should keep in view issues of income distribution and, at the same time, also endeavour to generate tax revenues to support government expenditure on public services and infrastructure development.

During the last four decades, GST has become an important instrument of indirect taxation with 130 countries having adopted this, resulting in one-fifth of the world's tax revenue. Tax reform in many of the developing countries has focused on moving to GST. Most of these countries have gained thus indicating that other countries would gain from its adoption too. For a developing economy like India, it is desirable to become more competitive and efficient in its resource usage. Apart from various other policy instruments, India must pursue taxation policies that would maximise its economic efficiency and minimise distortions and impediments to efficient allocation of resources, specialisation, capital formation and international trade.

Traditionally, India's tax regime relied heavily on indirect taxes including customs and excise. Revenue from indirect taxes was the major source of tax revenue till tax reforms were initiated during the nineties. The major argument put forth for heavy reliance on indirect taxes was that India's majority of population was poor and thus widening the base of direct taxes had inherent limitations. Another argument for reliance on indirect taxes was that agricultural income was not subjected to central income tax and there were administrative difficulties involved in collecting taxes.

The framework of value added tax (VAT), recognized as GST in several countries, has been one of the major development in taxation structures worldwide. More than 135 countries adopted the GST/VAT framework effectively. With the Indian economy getting more and more globalised, introduction of an integrated goods and services tax (GST) to replace the existing multiple tax structures of Central and State taxes is not only desirable but also vital in the emerging economic environment. The implementation of GST would ensure that India provides a tax regime that is almost similar to the rest of the world. It will also improve the international cost competitiveness of native goods and services. According to a report by the National Council of Applied Economic Research, GST is expected to increase economic growth by 0.9 percent to 1.7 percent and exports are expected to increase by 3.2 percent to 6.3 percent.

GST in India

GST is also known as value added tax (VAT) in few countries. GST/VAT is a consumption based tax wherein the basic principle is to tax the value addition at each business stage. To achieve this, tax paid on purchases is allowed as a set off/credit against liability on output/income.

GST is levied on all transactions of goods and services. Thus, in principle, GST should not differentiate between goods and services. Internationally, GST was first introduced in France and now more than 130 countries have introduced GST. Most of the countries, depending on their own socio-economic formation, have introduced national level GST or dual GST.

An important implication of GST is that it would reduce tax burden on producers and foster growth through greater production. Manufacturing is a costly business under the current tax system wherein a producer has to pay taxes not only on raw material procurement, but also on the final receipts from the sale of goods. This double taxation prevents manufacturers from producing to their optimum capacity and retards growth. GST, on the other hand, would take care of this problem by providing tax credit to the manufacturer. Basically, the tax already paid by him will be deducted from his final sale tax receipts and he would only have to pay the difference, i.e. for the value added to the product by him.

Also, due to absence of tax credits applicability for inter-State transactions, a manufacturer producing in one State has to pay taxes on sale of those goods in other States as well. This adds to their cost and leads to lower productivity. The various tax barriers such as check posts and toll plazas lead to a lot of wastage for perishable items being transported, a loss that translated into major costs through higher need of buffer stocks and warehousing costs as well. A single taxation system could eliminate this roadblock for them.

A single taxation on producers would also translate into a lower final selling price for the consumer. Currently, for a customer, the tax burden of goods is anywhere between 25-30 percent while the GST proposes a tax rate of 18 percent in the first year of implementation and would be brought down over the second year and in later years to come. The consumer would not only be able to purchase more goods with the same amount of money, but he would also look to buy more, thereby encouraging the market demand. Also, there will be more transparency in the system as the customers would know exactly how much taxes they are being charged and on what base.

Key Features of GST in India

GST is different from the current tax structure in many ways. Currently, taxes treat goods and services differently. Goods attract excise at the manufacturing level and VAT at the time of sale. In contrast, services attract only one levy i.e. services tax on taxable services. This distinction, in GST regime, would lose its importance as both goods and services would be treated as par for taxing purposes. GST is a consumption based tax levied on sale, manufacture and consumption on goods and services at a national level. This tax will be a substitute for all indirect taxes levied by the States and the Central government.

GST would add to government revenues by widening the tax base. Until now, services had been exempted from taxes. GST, however, brings them under the purview of taxation as well. This would eliminate tax evasion by corporations that escape taxes by bundling their goods along with services or whose products fall on the borderline of a good and a service, such as software products. Also, GST provides credits for the taxes paid by producers earlier in the goods/services chain. This would encourage these producers to buy raw material from different registered dealers. This would bring in more and more vendors and suppliers under the purview of taxation and reduce the ambiguity of the existing unorganised sector.

The GST will be levied on the import of goods and services into the country. Export and direct taxes like income tax, corporate tax and capital gain will not be affected by the GST. GST would apply to all goods other than crude petroleum, motor spirit, diesel, aviation turbine fuel and natural gas. It would apply to all services barring a few yet to be specified. A transaction in goods and services for a consideration would attract CGST and SGST. Also, the State Government now gets the power to tax services and Central Government gets the power to levy tax at the distribution and retail level.

To the extent feasible, uniform procedure for collection of both Central GST and State GST would be prescribed in the respective legislation for Central GST and State GST. Each taxpayer would be allotted a PAN-linked taxpayer identification number with a total of 13/15 digits. This would bring the GST PAN linked system in line with the prevailing PAN-based system for income tax, facilitating data exchange and taxpayer compliance. The taxpayer would need to submit common format for periodical returns, to both the concerned Central and

State GST authorities.

The proposed tax system will take the form of "dual GST" which is concurrently levied by the Central and State governments. In a dual GST regime, all the transactions of goods and services would attract two levies i.e. CGST (Central GST), which will be levied and collected by the Centre, and SGST (State GST), which will be levied and collected by the State. Besides, there will be IGST (Integrated GST) which will be levied by Central Government on inter-State supply of goods and services.

Many taxes would be subsumed under the GST. GST would be levied on all the transactions of goods and services made for a consideration. This new levy would replace almost all of the indirect taxes. In particular, it would replace the following indirect taxes:

At the Central level, the following taxes will be subsumed:

1. Central excise duty (including additional duties of excise).
2. Service tax.
3. CVD (levied on imports in lieu of excise duty).
4. SACD (levied on imports in lieu of VAT).
5. Central sales tax.
6. Excise duty levied on medicinal and toiletries preparations.
7. Surcharges and cesses.

At State level, the following taxes will be subsumed:

1. VAT/sales tax.
2. Entertainment tax (unless it is levied by the local bodies).
3. Luxury tax.
4. Taxes on lottery, betting and gambling.
5. Entry tax not in lieu of octroi.
6. Cesses and surcharges.

Administration: CGST and IGST will be administered by the Central Government and SGST will administered by the respective State government.

Law Relating to GST: In GST regime, there will be 1 CGST law and 31 SGST laws for each of the States including two Union Territories and one IGST law governing inter-State supplies of goods and services.

Rate of Tax: Determining a revenue neutral rate for GST will be a difficult task because all the States would be required to reach a consensus on it. It has been proposed to adopt a two rate structure, a lower rate for necessary items and items of basic importance and a standard rate for goods in general. There will also be a special rate for precious metals and a list of exempted items. For Central GST relating to goods, there might be a two rate structure, in conformity with the levels of rate with the State GST. For taxation of services, there may be a single rate for both Central GST and State GST.

While there is a consensus on the nature of levies that shall be subsumed in the GST, however, there is no consensus on the final GST rate. It has been recommended in the Chief Economic Advisor's Report (December 2015), that the GST regime should have a dual rate structure—low GST rate of approximately 12 percent on merit goods (e.g. essential commodities), and standard GST rate of approximately 18 percent on other goods. That apart, it is expected that there may be a higher GST rate of approximately 40 percent on a few demerit goods (like tobacco, aerated beverages, etc.), lower GST rate of approximately 2 percent on bullions, and exemption from GST on a few select goods. Over and above GST, there is a proposal to levy 1 percent additional tax on all inter-State supply of goods, which is non-creditable and will be retained by the selling State.

Inter-State Transactions in GST: All the inter-State transactions of goods and services would attract IGST (which would be CGST plus SGST). The inter-State seller will pay IGST on value addition after adjusting available credit of IGST, CGST, and SGST on his purchases. The exporting State will transfer to the Centre, the credit of SGST used in payment of IGST. The importing dealer will claim credit of IGST while discharging his output tax liability in his own State. The Centre will transfer to the importing State, the credit of IGST used in payment of SGST.

Objectives of GST

One of the main objectives of GST would be to eliminate the cascading impact of taxes on production and distribution cost of goods and services. The exclusion of cascading effects i.e. tax on tax will significantly improve the competitiveness of original goods and services which leads to beneficial impact for the GDP growth. GST will widen the tax base, improve tax compliance, remove existing unhealthy competition among States and re-distribute the burden of taxation equitably among manufacturing and services.

1. GST will ensure uniformity of taxes across the States, regardless of place of manufacture or distribution.
2. GST would integrate the tax base and allow seamless flow of input tax credit across the value chain of goods and services which will lead to reduced cost of goods and services.
3. GST environment would lead to improved disclosure of economic transactions which may have a positive impact on direct tax collections also.
4. The average tax burden on companies will fall which will reduce the costs of Indian goods and services in the international market and give boost to Indian exports.
5. GST also removes the custom duties applicable on exports. This will have major implications for the Indian economy—making exports tax-free would spur trade for our economy. Our competitiveness in foreign markets would increase on account of lower cost of transaction while the imports will be taxed same as domestic goods and services.
6. It will mitigate cascading and double taxation and enable better compliance through the lowering of overall tax burden on goods and services.
7. Overall, it will result in increased revenue for the Centre as the tax collection system becomes more transparent, making tax evasion difficult.

Benefits of GST

1. Easy compliance.
2. Removal of cascading.
3. Improved competitiveness for Central and State Governments.
4. Simple and easy to administer.
5. Better controls on leakage.
6. Consolidation of tax base.
7. Higher revenue efficiency for the consumer.
8. Single and transparent tax proportionate to the value of goods and services.
9. Reduction in prices.

Implementation of GST

In the past, the Government quite a few times announced the date to introduce GST and the said date has been postponed again and again. Earlier, the date for introduction of GST was April 2010, then it became April 2011 and then April 2012 and so on.

With the passage of the Bill in Rajya Sabha on August 3, 2016, it now seems that the GST would see the light of the day in the near future. Having said the above, the following important steps show that the Government is actively working on GST:

- 122nd Constitutional Amendment for GST has already been passed by the Lok Sabha.
- Contract to manage IT infrastructure has already been awarded to Infosys.
- The Act passed in accordance with the provisions of Article 368 of the Constitution, is to be ratified by more than half of the State legislatures.

Indian Prime Minister Shri Narendra Modi and Finance Minister Shri Arun Jaitley have repeatedly assured that the new proposed date of April 1, 2017, shows that the Government is committed to the introduction of GST.

Conclusion

GST is a single national uniform tax levied across India on all goods and services. GST, one of the most significant reforms introduced in the history of the Indian fiscal evolution, is likely to come into effect in 2017. GST is expected to have a far reaching impact, much beyond taxes on business, economy and the society.

Globally, GST is acknowledged as a progressive tax regime, with inbuilt efficiencies to broaden the tax base, decrease cascading effect and reduce revenue leakages. The proposed GST in India is expected to bring in uniform tax rates and provisions to simplify the compliance requirements across the country, supported by automated systems and processes. A well designed GST structure can foster common market and economic growth.

India is expected to adopt a dual GST model where the central and state governments will levy GST simultaneously, on a common taxable value, on the supply of goods and services. However, in the case of imports and inter-State supplies, an IGST (Integrated GST) shall be levied by the Central government. The proposed GST will subsume most of the existing central and state taxes on the supply of goods and services including central excise, service tax, State level value added tax (VAT) and other local levies on goods.

While there is a consensus on the nature of levies that shall be subsumed in the GST, however, there is no consensus on the final GST rate. With GST, there will be a significant shift from origin-based taxation to a destination-based tax structure impacting not only the operating business models but also the revenues of the Centre/States.

GST has the potential to impact cash flow, pricing, working capital, supply chain and IT systems and hence provides an opportunity to transform your business.

References

Empowered Committee of Finance Ministers (2009), "First Discussion Paper on Goods and Services Tax in India", The

Empowered Committee of State Finance Ministers, New Delhi.
Goods and Services Tax (GST): A Step Forward, available at: http://articles.economictimes.indiatimes.com/2013-08-13/news/41374977_1_services-tax-stategst-goods-and-services.
Gupta, Saurabh and Madhur Gupta (2014), "How Impossible GST Has Become Inevitable for India"? *Niveshak,* Volume 7, Issue 1, January, pp. 26-28.
Mukherjee, Pranab, Finance Minister of India, Speech at the Union Budget 2010-11, February 26, 2010, available at: http://www.thehindu.com/business/Econo my/article113901.ece.
Seventy Third Report of Standing Committee on Finance (2012-2013), available at: http://www.prsindia.org/uploads/media/Constitution%20115/GST%20SC%20Repo rt.pdf.
Vasanthagopal, R. (2011), "GST in India: A Big Leap in the Indirect Taxation System", *International Journal of Trade, Economics and Finance*, Volume 2, No. 2, April.
"What is GST (Goods and Services Tax)"? (2013), available at: http://www.moneycontrol.com/smementor/mentorade/budget-2013/what-is-gstgoods-and-services-tax-827592.html.

4

Goods and Services Tax: A Breakthrough

Dharmveer and Renu Verma

Goods and services tax (GST) would be a significant breakthrough in the history of tax reform in India that would replace all indirect taxes levied by Central as well as the State governments and transform into a uniform tax system on the line of "one nation-one tax" system. After the implementation, it is supposed to do away with a majority of shortcomings present in the current tax regime.

The GST will simplify the present tax regime, will be helpful in removing the cascading effect, and is expected to increase efficiency in tax collection which prevails in the current tax system. Also, it will increase tax revenue as it widens the tax base and will benefit taxpayers as it will reduce the overall rate by incorporating all the goods and services into taxation.

The GST will foster economic growth by expanding net export through improvement in competitiveness internationally and providing favourable investment environment to global investors as well as domestic manufacturers and producers. The introduction of GST will expand sector-specific growth such as agriculture and industry through the reduction in overall price level; it will increase real income of masses and would be helpful in reducing poverty and providing employment.

Introduction

In the previous decade, despite the unfavourable global economic as well as political condition, Indian economy performed well in comparison to leading world economies as well as with regards to other emerging economies. Currently, with favourable macroeconomic conditions such as high gross fixed capital formation, high savings rate etc., India remains an attractive destination for foreign investment, though it needs to further improve and provide sufficient foundation to achieve higher economic growth in future.

However, these favourable conditions require certain policy reforms in different sectors of the economy. Tax reform is one of them which require urgent attention to foster economic growth in the Indian economy.

The goods and services tax (GST) would be a significant breakthrough in the history of tax reform in India that would replace all indirect taxes levied by Central as well as State governments and transform into a uniform tax system on the line of "one nation-one tax" system. After the implementation, it is supposed to do away with the majority of shortcomings existing in the present tax regime (Mukherjee, 2015).

According to various estimates, the goods and services tax has the potential to push India's gross domestic product by 1 to 2 percent.

The main objective of this paper is to describe the main features of the proposed goods and services tax and how it would be an improvement over the current taxation system. Prior to answering these questions, this paper would give a brief insight into the present indirect tax structure in India and what are the major shortcomings in this tax structure? The subsequent part of this paper would discuss the possible impacts of GST on the Indian economy and its various sectors.

Present Indirect Tax Structure in India

An indirect tax consists of four components, i.e. service tax; value added tax, central excise, and customs law which are paid by the service provider on behalf of service receiver for incidence borne by the taxpayer.

Service Tax: Service tax is levied, collected and appropriated by the Union government as per Article 268A and directives on it are given by Chapter 5 of the Finance Act, 1994. There are various loopholes in services tax which are discussed below.

States are disallowed from levying service tax resulting from an undesirable impact on the flexibility of state tax revenue. Service sector share in terms of real GDP in India has outdone agriculture and industry compared to other industrialized nations with a 56.2 percent contribution in 2014-15. As States do not have the power to levy this tax, this growing sector gives no benefit to States thereby resulting on their reliance on other sources.

Another issue involved with service tax is the difficulty in calculation of taxable value of service tax where both services and goods are involved in a transaction. Examples include: (a) work contract, where transfer of property is taken as goods and value of services include labour charges for execution of work, consumable costs (electricity, fuel, water), designing charges, architect fees etc. Even though a simplified scheme can be used at the option of assesses for calculating value of goods and services, it however makes the procedure time consuming and leads to red tapism. Also, CENVAT credit of excise duty or cess is not available on inputs used in executing a work contract; (b) Software and copyright are intangible goods but are often supplied according to service contract arrangements. Canned software is taken as goods and onsite development of software as service being a part of information technology software but if it is transferred to the customer on a CD, it is considered as goods; (c) Lease finance cases have also faced disputes vis-à-vis leasing of equipment to the lessee without transferring the possession and control and would be considered as a taxable service or deemed as sale of goods.

Every year, services are amended where some are added to or removed from the negative list and some are added to the declared services. This leads to ambiguity and increases the complexity.

Value Added Tax: It is a multiple stage tax levied by a State on value added to a product and was implemented with effect from April 1, 2005 replacing the sales tax system. VAT calculation is done after deducting input tax credit i.e. set-off for tax paid earlier, to reduce the cascading effect.

Limitations of VAT are as follows:

- It increases accounting and administrative costs as a number of dealers dealing under VAT goes up and working capital increases as tax is levied at multi levels leading to higher litigation and higher compliance cost which creates anti-business environment.
- State VAT base suffers: VAT doesn't cover all goods and services that go into final consumption as it extends only till the retail stage.
- Floor rate: States have two basic rates; 12.5 percent (general rate) and 4 percent (reduced rate) known as floor rate (minimum rate) which is supposed to be applied uniformly but the State will have no freedom of choice to go above the prescribed rate against what the floor rate implies.
- Tax evasion is possible by issuing the fake invoice to claim tax credit.
- Threshold limit below which VAT is not applicable differs from one State to another making the procedure complex.

CENVAT or Excise Duty: It is levied by the Central government as per Entry 84 of List 1 of the Seventh Schedule of the Constitution, on all manufactured goods or goods produced in India except on alcohol for human consumption, narcotic, opium for which the State governments levy excise duty. However, if they (alcohol for human consumption, narcotics, and opium) are covered under Medicinal and Toilet Preparations Act, then the Central government has the power to levy tax. Major items on which central excise duty is levied include sugar, cotton, mill cloth, tobacco, motor spirit, matches, cement etc.

Shortcomings associated with it are explained below:

- Definitional issue i.e. what constitutes manufacturing.
- Raises inventory cost: States levy entry tax/octroi when goods pass through States resulting in the delay in passage of goods at the borders and thereby increasing the inventory cost.

- CENVAT base is narrow: This is happening because of conditional and unconditional exemptions which the government has reintroduced by giving concessions to various sectors like agricultural implements, tractors, health care, hand tools, meat, poultry products etc.
- Complexity: It exists because of irrational structure and multiple rates.

Customs Law: It is derived from the ancient practice whereby when one merchant entered into another kingdom and he had to give a gift to get permission to sell goods. It includes duties levied on imports and exports like countervailing duty, education cess, anti-dumping duty, protective duty, national calamity contingent duty etc.

Shortcomings of customs law are as under:

- Discourage domestic value addition: Inverted duty structure means making manufactured goods uncompetitive against finished product imports in the domestic market as finished goods are taxed at lower rates than raw materials or intermediate products.
- Compliance issue.

Gains from Goods and Services Tax

The present indirect taxation system in India entails the need to levy a number of indirect taxes on businesses and individuals. Under the present taxation system, certain problems arise, such as problem of double taxation, multiple layers of tax that increase the overall tax rate, tax evasion thereby lowering the tax base that results in significant decline in tax revenue and which also proves to be economically inefficient. The present tax regime has many layers of indirect taxes which are levied on producers and manufacturers that motivate them to employ tax evasion techniques to escape from paying tax on their profits. The consequent result is a significant decline in tax revenue for the government and sub-optimal level of production of goods and services.

The possible gains from GST after implementation can be

counted as under:

1. It would widen the tax base and consequently the tax revenues for both the Central as well as State governments.
2. It will reduce the distortions in the economy through a more comprehensive tax credit.
3. It will enhance the competitiveness of domestic product in the global market by relieving domestic consumption tax on export.
4. It will also ensure greater regional integrity by getting rid of inter-State sales tax and having a destination based tax that will create a national market by removing inter-State trade barriers.
5. It will significantly reduce the compliance cost for taxpayers by simplifying and harmonizing the tax structure and by making the administration uniform.

Indian economy had achieved a remarkable GDP growth in the last decade despite unfavourable global economic conditions. Currently, macroeconomic variables are stable to achieve a sustained and high economic growth but these favourable conditions are coupled with few policy challenges in various sectors. Among them, tax reform is a very important and necessary step to foster growth and overall development of the economy.

Currently, while the world's most industrialised and other emerging economies are facing old age problem as their working force is shrinking and these countries will be having greater dependency ratios, India has the largest workforce at present and in next two decades a large chunk of youth is going to join the workforce. To harness this opportunity—called the demographic dividend—we need to work on two fronts. On one side we need to enhance their skills through comprehensive training programmes and by providing qualitative education, and on the other hand, we have to increase employment opportunities by increasing our economic activities. As per the 'Ease of Doing Business

Report, 2015', India ranks 142 which depicts the problems of starting business in India (World Bank, 2015).

The proposed GST is a tax reform which would facilitate investment by improving the investment climate, much needed to advance economic growth. GST will reduce the tax burden by reducing tax rate as well as well by reducing or mitigating the problem of double taxation which prevails in the current taxation system. The reduced tax burden will encourage domestic as well global manufacturers to increase economic activity that would result in more employment generation and an increase in income (World Bank, 2015).

Potential benefits for the stakeholders are as under:

- Reduction in multiplicity of taxes.
- Mitigation of cascading effect.
- Efficient naturalizations of taxes, especially for exports.
- Development of common national market or common economic market.
- Simpler tax regime with fewer rates and exemptions.
- Increase in cost competitiveness for domestic industries with reduction in tax cost as also the reduced cost of compliance.

A simpler tax system with widened tax base would improve compliance and tax collections thereby increasing the revenue of government for promoting the efficient allocation of resources. Further it would lead to improved input productivity and hence income and overall production in the economy.

The proposed GST will also enhance the domestic savings due to mitigation of cascading effects, contributing to increase in availability of funds that can be used to finance much needed investment in infrastructure development and under-funded social sector (Government of India, 2015).

GST would reduce the cost of goods and services through the elimination of cascading effects of taxes that will reduce overall prices. A fall in overall prices would lead to increase in consumers' real income and purchasing power. An increase in real income gives incentive either to consume more or to save. Both will have positive impacts on the Indian economy by increasing aggregate demand or by increasing funds available for the investment.

The proposed GST is supposed to reduce the burden of tax on both consumers and producers through reduced tax rate. The reduced tax burden will increase the domestic consumption by increasing the purchasing power of the consumers, especially the fixed income group and middle class. As consumption is an important part of aggregate demand in an economy, especially in the case of the Indian economy, it will increase the aggregate demand in the economy and a higher aggregate demand would lead to higher employment and consequently a high level of production.

The other significant component of aggregate demand is investment which is also a function of the investment climate and domestic savings. The proposed GST would facilitate the investment environment in the economy by simplifying the tax structure. A complex tax structure and double taxation increase the cost of doing business that disincentives investor to allocate resources efficiently, consequently leading to sub-optimal level of potential production. Under the GST regime, both domestic as well as global investors will get incentives to invest more in Indian economy.

The proposed GST will also facilitate investment through increased savings in the economy as it will reduce the overall prices and tax burden of the population. The reduced prices increase the real income of the people and they will intend to do more savings. Hence, a higher level of investment can be financed by increased savings in the economy.

Government expenditure which is also an important factor of aggregate demand depends on the fiscal capacity of any government. The government expenditure plays a very important role in promoting economic growth, particularly during the times of depression. The fiscal capacity of any government depends on the tax revenues as well as mobilization of resources from nontax resources. Currently, the tax-GDP ratio in India is small at 16.5 percent of the GDP as compared to Asian countries and OECD countries (Economic Survey, 2016).

Under the current tax regime, due to multiple layers of indirect taxes of States as well as Central government, the problem of double taxation and due to the practice of tax evasion techniques by producers or manufacturers, it results in low tax revenues.

Under GST, the tax would be levied on both goods and services, which would increase the tax base of both Central as well as State governments. The reduced rate of tax under GST would also increase the total number of taxpayers. The increased number of taxpayers and a comparatively larger tax base would result in overall tax revenues thereby strengthening government's fiscal capacity (Government of India, 2015).

Even though the Indian economy is much dependent on domestic demand, export demand is nowhere less, becoming a significant part of the aggregate demand. The GST would remove all the excise and customs duties on domestic products. A tax-free domestic product is more competitive in global markets, expanding our export demand while at the same time imports would be taxed as other goods and services which make imports expensive consequently reducing the import demand. Therefore, the net effect of GST would be an increase in aggregate demand. This would lead to a higher level of economic activity and higher level of employment and production.

Conclusion

Goods and services tax as a part of tax reform in India will subsume all the indirect taxes levied at the level of Centre as well as in the States. After the implementation, it is supposed to resolve all the shortcomings prevailing in the existing tax regime and would have remarkable impacts on the Indian economy as it would be helpful in sustaining and achieving a higher growth rate. It would be helpful in harnessing the demographic dividend by creating a favourable environment for domestic as well as global manufacturers and by increasing the fiscal capacity to spend on much needed infrastructure sector and under-funded social sector in India.

References

Deepa, K.S. and D. Raguram (2015), "Goods and Service Tax: The Introduction Process", W.P. No. 2015-03-01, Research and Publication, IIMA.

FICCI (2013), "Towards the GST: An Approach Paper", PRS Legislative Research, New Delhi.

First Discussion Paper on Goods and Services Tax in India (2009), The Empowered Committee of State Finance Ministers, New Delhi.

Government of India (2016), "Economic Survey", Ministry of Finance, Government of India.

Government of India (2015), "An Insight of Goods and Service tax (GST) in India", Tax Research Department, The Institute of Cost Accountants of India.

Mukherjee, S. (2015), "Present State of Goods and Service Tax (GST) Reform in India", Working Paper No. 2015-154, NIPFP, New Delhi.

Poddar, S. and E. Ahmad (2009), "GST Reforms and Intergovernmental Considerations in India", Asia Research Centre, Working Paper No. 26, LSE, London.

Vasanthagopal, R. (2011), "GST in India: A Big Leap in the Indirect Taxation System", *International Journal of Trade, Economics and Finance*, Vol. 2, No. 2, April.

5

Comparing GST with Current Indirect Taxes

Jasmine Jha

Goods and services tax (GST) is a radical amendment suggested in India's indirect tax system. Presently, the Constitution empowers Central Government to levy excise duty on manufacturing and service tax on supply side and State Government to levy value added tax (VAT). This gives autonomy to both Centre and the States. In addition to this, Central sales tax (CST) is levied on inter-State sale of goods by the Central Government but collected and retained by the State government. This apart, there are is plethora of other indirect taxes which are also involved. All these reasons and more have made our indirect tax system very complex. The major issue which is currently faced by India is *tax on tax*. This has led to tax cascading which artificially inflates values leading to high prices or inflation.

There are more issues involved with our tax system today. GST does helps in sorting these problems but it has its own limitations which need to be taken care of. For example, introduction of GST will lead to revenue losses for the State governments. In this paper, we compare our current indirect tax system with the GST. Is GST an improvement over our indirect tax system or its drawbacks eclipse the advantages received from the new advised system of GST? The objective of this paper is to find out if the gains from GST are greater than the losses. We would also be discussing a little about gains and losses from the proposed tax system. This study focuses on GST's effects and impacts on different sectors and the society.

Introduction

Taxes are an important source of revenue for the government. They are of two types viz. direct and indirect taxes. These have their sub-categories. In this paper, we focus on current indirect taxes and goods and services tax. As we know, the sub-division of indirect tax is going to be replaced by goods and services tax. In this paper, we are going to analyse its merits and demerits and other factors getting affected by this change of taxation policy.

Indirect taxes are when taxes are paid indirectly i.e. the incidence of tax falls on the ultimate consumer and the burden of tax is easily passed on. It is the tax levied on goods or services, rather on a person or an organization such as customs duty, excise duty, service tax etc. Taxes in India are levied by Central and State governments but some minor taxes are also levied by municipalities or the local council.

Good and services tax (GST) is being proposed via The Constitution Bill, 2014, which seeks to amend the Constitution of India to facilitate the introduction of GST in the country. The proposed amendments will confer powers to both Parliament and State Legislatures to make laws for levying GST on the supply of goods and services on the same transactions. It was introduced as a solution to "tax on tax" issue. In this paper, we will study what issues indirect taxes have in the current timeframe and how the introduction of GST will be used as a means to rectify these problems. Introduction of GST will have its own merits and demerits. This paper also touches upon them. It also tries to analyse which sectors will gain from the amendment and why?

Comparison

As we all know that taxes are an important source of revenue for the government, the division of tax system in the Indian economy is on the basis of direct tax and indirect tax. The objectives of a taxation system are as under:

1. Raising revenue: The government has to perform many functions for the purpose of welfare of the society. For this, taxation is an important source of revenue.
2. Regulation of consumption and production: Government

uses taxation system as a tool to regulate consumption and production of goods. For example, taxing tobacco will help in reduction in consumption or production of tobacco.

3. Encouraging domestic industries: High taxation on import of goods provides comparative advantage to domestic industries by either equalizing the price in the market or by giving the domestic industries the cost benefit.
4. Reducing income inequalities: It plays an important role to reduce income inequalities. This system takes the excess income from the rich and is used to provide social benefits to the poor. This method helps in reducing the gap between the affluent and the deprived.
5. The other important aspects are the development of backward regions, price stability, etc. The revenue collected by the government is used for the development of the society and also for providing basic necessities to the deprived population. On the other hand, globalization has made all the markets vulnerable to price changes. Since India is still a developing country and any extreme fluctuation affects our economy in the worst way possible, therefore to reduce these fluctuations, the government uses the taxing system and tries to keep prices stable in the domestic economy.

Since taxing system is very complex not just for the consumers but also for the government, few canons were given by some economists to make this system easy and workable with fewer amounts of hurdles faced by both sectors of the society. Few of the important canons are discussed below:

1. Canon of equality: A person should pay according to his/her ability to pay.
2. Canon of certainty: The payer should be well informed of each and every aspect of taxing policy which involves every details of the payment of each and every kind of taxation.
3. Canon of economy: Cost of collecting tax should not be more than the revenue and should be economical.

4. The other canons include, canon of productivity, canon of elasticity, canon of simplicity and canon of diversity.

Table 5.1 gives the break-up of tax revenue of the Central government for the year 2013-14.

Table 1: Break-up of the Tax Revenue of the Central Government: 2013-14

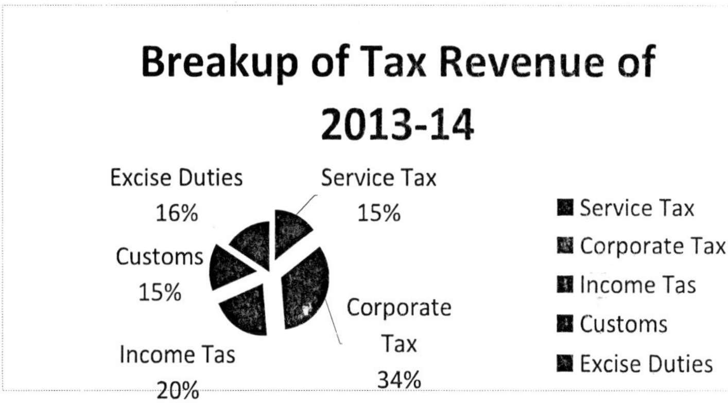

Indirect taxes are taxes which are levied on goods and services and it includes excise duty, customs duty, service tax and securities transaction tax. In India, Central or State governments are capable of enforcing laws in order to control indirect taxes. Since almost all activities ranging from manufacturing to consumption are subjected to indirect taxation, therefore it has an effect in all business areas.

To overcome the existing demerits of the indirect tax system, GST is proposed to be introduced. GST fulfils the canons of taxation, specially the canon of economy which is not fulfilled by the current indirect tax system. The major reason why GST is being introduced is to resolve the problem of "taxes on taxes". This is better explained using an example. Let's say X is selling a commodity to Y after charging sales tax and the same commodity is sold by Y to Z after charging sales tax again on it. In this situation, Y has transferred his tax liability to Z. This situation leads to tax on tax scenario.

On the other hand, GST model is supposed to subsume most (if not all) of the existing Central and State taxes on the supply of goods and services, including excise duty, sales tax, VAT, etc. India shall adopt the dual GST model which means that both Central and State governments will administer it. It has three divisions to it which are: (SGST) State GST which will be collected by the State. (CGST) Central GST will be collected by the Central government and (IGST) Integrated GST which will be collected by the Central government.

The next step is to know the working of GST. If the sale is made in one State and then the resale is made in the same State, then CGST and SGST will be applied. The Central and the State Governments will get their share according to their specified percentage. When the sale is made in a State and resale in another State then IGST will be applied, which will be collected by the Central government.

This new tax regime is stated to be less complex in comparison to the present taxing system. It will make various business decisions tax neutral. This ensures that commercial efficiencies are not compromised on account of tax imperatives. This system is said to provide uniformity in tax system across States with minimal cascading of taxes and widening of the tax net. Since the tax rates will be uniformed throughout the country but to provide fiscal autonomy, there will be provision of tax band over and above the floor rates of CGST, SGST and IGST. The major issue in introducing GST was the loss of revenue by the States. But the solution referred for it is that the Centre will compensate States for their losses for a few years.

The potential changes by this taxing system would be effective tax rates for supplies and purchases. Transactions which are currently exempted from tax may become liable to GST but it will eventually lead to fall in prices in the long-run. This will make our economy more competitive. Under the current tax regime, the cumulative rate of tax on goods is around 20-22 percent and in services it is only 14 percent. The overall rate is 25-30 percent. But the introduction of GST will bring it down to 18-20 percent.

GST will impact different sectors differently at present. In the agriculture sector, food is currently exempted from CENVAT; however, with the introduction of GST it will double the tax burden on food. Thus, prices in agricultural sector are expected to rise and the overall effect will be negative. In the manufacturing sector, the positives include full credit of tax on inter-State sale which will lead to fall in procurement and production cost and moreover credit of import duties will make imports cheaper. GST will eliminate entry tax which is considered as a burden for the manufacturing sector. The negatives of this regime are job work transaction and stock transfers which are currently not taxed and will be taxed in the new regime. It will also increase the cost of procurement from 12 percent to around 20 percent. Positive impacts are expected in the textile and pharmaceuticals sector. Neutral impact will be seen in roads, hotel and construction sectors.

As we have studied above, we find out that GST resolves most of the problems being dealt in the current indirect system. It prominently has an overall positive impact in the economy. All of these positives will be realized only after its correct implementation otherwise the problems which will arise will be more difficult to deal with. GST will simplify the process but losses which will be incurred during the implementation of the new taxing system should be taken into consideration and should be worked on.

Conclusion

The study finds out that GST model which is being implemented in India is actually providing a better solution for the issues faced by the current indirect taxation system. It is helping in making our economy more competitive domestically and in the foreign market. This is due to the unified and lower tax levels leading to lower costs incurred by the manufacturing sector. It will give boost to manufacturing sector but possibly harm the agriculture sector. However, this model will only be effective if and only if the model is implemented correctly and there should be transparency in the system with appropriate compensations allotted to the organizations and States which are going to sacrifice a part of their revenue due to the implementation of the new tax regime.

References

A Study on Proposed Goods and Services Tax (GST) Framework in India, available at: http://www.caaa.in/Image/23ugsthb.pdf.

Arvind Subramanian (2015), "GST impact on Various Sectors", Summary of the Committee Report.

Chheda T. and K. Shah, *"GST Impacts and Expectations of Industry*", available at: cvocaassociation.com/resource/image/GST_Impact_Expectation_of%20_Industry.pdf.

Concept Note on GST (2015), Department of Revenue, Ministry of Finance, Government of India, available at: http://dor.gov.in/gstintro.

Vivek Chowdhury (2011), "Taxes in India and the Advantages and Disadvantages of Direct Taxes and Indirect Taxes", available at: http://www.indiastudychannel.com/resources/140421-Taxes-India-advantages.aspx.

Part II:
GST: The Less Contested Problems

6

GST: The Less Explored Issues

Arun Kumar

Introduction of GST in the country is being billed as the biggest tax reform in India and a game changer. Unfortunately, many critical issues regarding the basic design of GST have not been discussed and remain unresolved.

GST has three important elements. First, combining together of taxes like, excise, sales, services, etc. It is said that seventeen taxes will be replaced by one and this will lead to ease of business. Second, the indirect taxes will be calculated on value addition and not the value of the good or service. This would remove the cascading effect of tax on tax and profit on tax. Finally, not only would the cascading effect of each of the taxes (excise, sales, services and so on) be removed but even that across these taxes would go. This would lead to a possible fall in prices, all else remaining the same. It is argued that this would lead to ease of doing business which could boost the growth of the economy.

Undoubtedly, there would be simplification in the tax regime faced by businesses but not as much as is being made out. There will be three taxes—CGST collected by the Centre, SGST collected by the States and an IGST on inter-State movements collected by the Centre. Further, under pressure from the States, alcohol, tobacco and petro goods are likely to be left out of the purview of the GST. So are electricity and real estate being left out of the GST net and will have separate taxes resulting in some cascading effect.

Further, since value addition is only a fraction of the value of a product, if the tax rate remains the same as earlier, the tax collection would fall. Thus, if the government is to collect the same amount of tax as in the earlier tax regime, it would have to raise the tax rate under VAT. This is called the revenue neutral rate (RNR) and could be pretty high. Further, tax will have to be collected at each stage of production and distribution. So, even if the tax rate is a common one, collection of the tax will still be complex.

Services did not have to pay sales tax but will now have to pay the SGST to the States hence their prices will rise. For instance, telephone calls, insurance, transportation, restaurants, etc. will become dearer. Further, one common tax rate will imply that all basic and essential goods prices will rise and even if some final goods prices fall, the rate of inflation will go up.

If the rate of inflation rises, demand in the economy would fall and the rate of growth will decline contrary to the argument by proponents of GST. To avoid this, the government will have to give up the RNR and fix lower rates of tax. But then the collection of tax will fall compared to the present and the States will suffer. The deficit of the Centre and the states will then rise. This is the worry of the States. If the Centre tries to compensate them for the fall in revenue, as it is promising to do so, then the Centre's deficit will rise even more which will create further problems.

These macroeconomic issues have not been debated or resolved in the rush to implement GST. Another ignored aspect is the interest of the small-scale and unorganized sectors.

Small-scale sector produces and sells locally so it would hardly benefit from a unified market. It is being exempted from the payment of GST and, therefore, would not be able to claim credit for any purchase from the organized sector and would be at a disadvantage. If it sells to the organized sector, it would not be able to provide the benefit of set-off and, therefore, it would have to cut prices or its sales would decline. A decline in the small and unorganized sector would reduce employment generation since it is an employment intensive sector.

Take the example of potato chips or envelope making where the large scale has displaced the cottage sector. Or, look at any 'haat' selling cheaper versions of products sold in the malls or regular shops. They are visited by the poor, the lower and the middle class who go there to buy cheap products supplied by the small and cottage sectors. Such products will also get displaced.

VAT is a difficult tax to implement since it requires keeping account of both the inputs (so as to claim set-off) and revenue from sales. The small-scale and the cottage sectors do not keep detailed accounts and cannot calculate how much VAT to pay. That is the reason, VAT requires computerization which the small and cottage sector are not able to afford.

Due to such difficulties, VAT could not be introduced in the 1970s. Indirect Tax Reform Committee in 1978 suggested MANVAT on manufacturing alone. This could not be implemented because of the existence of a very large unorganized sector in manufacturing. Long Term Fiscal Policy (LTFP) in 1986 suggested MODVAT which had to be introduced gradually till CENVAT replaced it a decade later. Difficulties are being swept under the carpet. It is these difficulties that would also undermine the claims that compliance would improve under VAT and that the black economy would decline.

GST by introducing one common rate for all States undermines fiscal federalism. Different States have different requirements. Needs of Maharashtra are different from those of Assam. The manufacturing States are worried about the loss of revenue due to change of tax from source to destination and to accommodate them, IGST is proposed. Even though the States have arrived at a consensus and given up their powers, undermining federalism will have long-term affects which will not be visible immediately. The local bodies, the third tier of the federal structure are entirely left out of the reckoning.

To conclude, the real problems with introduction of GST in India have not been addressed. The unorganized sector in India employs 93 percent of the workforce. The small and tiny units producing and selling locally would lose from a unified market which will benefit the large scale producers. This will aggravate under employment, distress in the farm sector and adversely impact the poorer States. No wonder GST is being strongly backed by large businesses—foreign and Indian. Just because VAT exists in more than a hundred nations is no reason that it would uniformly benefit all in India.

Finally, there are contradictions in the argument being made for GST. Tax-GDP ratio will rise if tax collection rises but then prices will rise, demand would fall and the economy would slow down. Contrarily, if RNR is given up, then the tax-GDP ratio will fall and States' resource position will deteriorate. The macroeconomic analysis shows that either way the government's arguments are contradictory.

References

The Tribune, August 24, 2015.

7

Some Thoughts on GST: A Victory of the Powerful Crony Lobbies for Further Marginalization of the Severely Marginalized Masses of India

Kamal Nayan Kabra

I have not made a detailed study of the nitty-gritty and minutiae of the proposed GST which is paraded as a major tax 'reform' in India. But a cursory understanding of it in terms of the overall context of Indian political economy in general and her fiscal system in particular along with the essential concept and supposed and much advertised rationale of GST are, to my mind, enough to give rise to a number of apprehensions. More specifically, it is so when fiscal policy in general and taxation measures in particular are viewed, howsoever fleetingly, from the point of view of really inclusive development (not as a cosmetic exercise of democratic deceit indulged in by the rich, powerful and famous in India as a widespread practice). It is some concession to reality that necessitates among the neo-liberals, a concern for inclusive development, of course following the lead provided by the World Bank. It is projected as a far-reaching corrective to the prevailing GDP-centric highly disequalizing and disempowering perspective of neo-liberal growth.

This kind of growth-manship, particularly owing to the prevailing neo-liberal ideological and narrow social commitments seem presently to take precedence on everything else—as can be seen from the competitive pursuit of so-called neo-liberal reforms by the two major contenders for political power in India. The latter is an exercise to do the same but with a different public face and in order to break the power monopoly of a single group of political classes, though both the groupings are operating with some loose intertwining with the top business bosses under our prevailing system of crony economic and political oligopoly!

Let it be clearly understood that the Indian fiscal system as it stands today surely demands a major overhaul. It neither serves the state in terms of adding to its autonomous power and capability to enable it to do what it professes (may be a part of the democratic allurements offered to the potential voters, which is a typical feature of most market mechanism and private corporate power driven open economies in the present era to supplement their single-track push for corporate profit inflation under the cover of various populist measures (ostensible pro-poor thrust based on the logic of both democratic vote mobilization and cheap labour imperative of the corporate businesses). These postures also hinge on the concerns of the MNCs as the most critical major centres of economic, financial and technological power and the military capabilities of the topmost hegemonic nation states and their geo-political and business satellites supporting Indian neo-liberal reforms.

The prevailing fiscal mechanism as it has evolved over the last almost seven decades fails the state to enable it to command a reasonably autonomous financial and operational space for openly and unambiguously follow what it upholds as its agenda in terms of its stated, as against the real, objectives of state policy. Even with huge resource mopping by privatization of the existing PSUs as also that of the vacuum created by withdrawal of public investment from key areas of the economy and thus reducing the demand for investible funds by the state, the state remains under severe pressure and has to go in for statutory fiscal discipline. As a result, we have a fiscally constrained state able to satisfy neither the big players entrusted with the agency role nor the people at large who are promised a better pace under the Sun. This is because the big guns always want the state on their side wholly and without reservations under the cloak of pursuit of high and increasing growth rates of GDP, of course by means of ever larger bottom line of their balance sheets.

Such a growth process is supposed to result from rising rate of investments by the local and foreign capital effectively funded directly or indirectly by transfer of resources from the general public (that is without the big money having to curtail its fast growing consumerist pursuits of wallowing in super luxuries and accumulation of precious valuables). Actually, it is the growth resulting from transfer of peoples resources, financial and real both (such as land, mineral resources, sources of water, forest resources with scant concern for global warming) which effectively are controlled and used up by the corporate giants by means of the overgrown and narrowly controlled financial sector entities. One can appreciate the reasons for the all out push for GST by both the government and businesses by factoring in the above outlined overall context.

Remember, the rising growth rate is propagated as the panacea for the country's bright and just future, as though in a highly skewed society everyone is taken on board by the growth process and that too in a fair and just manner. Can one say this expectation is realizable if not in a relevant short-run may be in the long-run? Do the growthmanship stalwarts ever stop for a moment to wonder whether it is a long-run during which the young aspirants in their millions can get a fair and just livelihood earning opportunities even during their working lives (something which has eluded an overwhelming majority so far after nearly seven decades of growth of GDP)? Or is it a long-run of the Keynesian variety in which we are all dead! Recall how the official statistics has stopped counting the total backlog of people without adequate and regular access to means of using their capabilities for earning an honest livelihood!

Why we mention this issue is because the state as provider of social and public goods and services, as a growth and development agency, promoter, regulator and planner and a just and fair democratic arbiter among various divergent and conflicting claims and counter-claims, has to make use of its powers, particularly the fiscal authority, to make development a real development of all and that too by at least controlling the spiral of worsening disparities and increasing decent employment opportunities to cope up with the annual sizeable additions to employable young persons. The large role is unconceivable without a strong, not necessarily large, presence of the state in the economy with a decisive voice over the use pattern and beneficiaries of the social resources, at least as a mediator to protect and promote the right to life and development with dignity of the historically socially adversely included majority of citizens presently sidelined owing to excessive fixation with the resource-use miser and relative capabilities rich privileged minority of citizens at the top echelons. Recall how the annual memoranda for the fiscal policy changes by the big organized capital to the fiscal authorities get translated in as short a time as possible into actual budget proposals and fiscal laws and the rest of the have-nots are left high and dry, except for the rephrased same old promises.

Let us cut short the overall qualitative context and come to hard facts. Despite huge pressing and overdue social-public tasks requiring an active state to create conditions in which the majority of people can develop their productive and social capabilities and contribute to the common task of producing the wherewithal for a good and quality life for everyone in a framework that reflects our values as enshrined in our Constitution. It is in this context that the GST proposal is making rounds as something that can do the trick where most all others, well known parts of the neo-liberal agenda, seem to have been less than successful. Or is it the nature of these reforms that they are never complete and a new element always presents itself as the old one is carried through.

Let us face some facts on the fiscal front. We have one of the lowest tax-GDP ratio (hovering around 10 percent as far as the Union budget goes). Thus, in every single task that is to be performed by public expenditure directly and immediately benefiting the general public to equip them with both civic amenities (in villages and small towns and for getting rid of the stigma of slums prior to the extravagant spread of super luxurious amenities in a few pockets of the deluxe localities with enormously expensive houses and villas) has been an object of criminal neglect. See the data collected by the Socio-economic Caste Census (SECC), 2011 and you would shed a few genuine tears at the outcomes produced by perverse allocations of our scarce fiscal resources.

Similarly, the production capabilities enhancing public goods and services, including even public health, elementary and secondary education in good quality schools giving better facilities to those who have been the victims of centuries of accumulated neglect and exclusion, let alone paved intra-village streets with sanitation, lighting facilities and security of lives, limb and human dignity against the pervasive social authoritarianism based on caste, gender, access to public goods and equal protection of law rather than fancy showy projects. Even what is supposed to serve the general adversely included masses, such as building private toilets has been prioritized without first ensuring water supply or even a structure with a roof that can be treated as a house except by default.

On the contrary, huge sums are spent driven by international demonstration effect on prestigious, latest technology-based showy facilities whose location and pricing simply rule out the majority of people from their use, let alone benefiting from them, even in terms of construction labour or as maintenance staff. The short point is in the budgetary allocations of public expenditure there are no traces of the principle of progressive dispensation which requires relatively higher priority, a democratically ordained priority the needs and requirements of the common citizens to enable them to join the mainstream of social-economic and political life of the community.

What such a pro-people, democratic restructuring of the fiscal policies call for is a quantum jump in the size of the budget, a rise in tax-GDP ratio on par with the most developing third world and other countries offering a secure and better life to those at the lowest rungs of their respective social pyramids. It is something which cannot be accomplished by relying on indirect taxes as the main and bigger source of public revenue and letting the rich and the super rich, especially the corporate sector entities go practically scotch free, especially in an overall sense, taking note of both the bounties and spurs offered to them as also under-priced and disproportionately heavily funded public and quasi-public goods and services excessively catering to the needs of the modern, organized corporate and metropolitan services and facilities and access to the natural and heritage resources.

Yes, such things may make India look an isolated island compared to the rich West and even some of the third world which followed and follows in the footsteps of a mimetic, exogenously determined pattern of socio-economic and scientific changes. Real nationalism, people's nationalism, requires giving highest priority to the weak and the vulnerable in the country in our millions of villages and slums as these are the people who constitute India of today and tomorrow and are the real solid bases of national power, pride and purpose.

Compared to some such imperatives, the GST simply appears as a means of doing more of the same which has become our bane. It fails to improve our tax-GDP ratio, particularly its bias against indirect taxes and against the common man and woman. Treating the grossly unequal as equal in terms of tax liabilities, whether on goods and/or services, is among the worse ways of perpetuating inequalities. It becomes still more deplorable when the unequal position/ location/capabilities and potential for social good of the producers or service providers is simply treated as irrelevant when it comes to collecting taxes from the goods and services produced/provided by them. Actually it seems the words, concepts and concerns for matters related to equality among citizens have been simply obliterated from the mindset of the neo-liberal policy establishment.

Like in any large and modern society, we have in India vast and glaring disparities not only in the level of consumption, but more sharply and significantly in the commodities composition or the pattern of consumption, the hierarchy of needs and preferences underlying them and the ease and regularity of the assured and affordable availability of the articles of consumption, with or without greatly fluctuating prices, are matters which get buried under the heavy weight of a uniform all-India pattern of taxation as the hall mark of GST. We require a pattern of commodity taxation which differentiates between the rich man goods and services and the poor persons goods and services, positive health and welfare promoting pattern of consumption as also one that penalizes the dependence on demerit goods and services, say for example, between bus fares and taxi fares or taxi fares in super deluxe luxury cars and the run-of the mill ordinary taxis or air travel and super luxurious train services and so on examples can be easily multiplied.

Such a people sensitive, justice and fair play-centric pattern and system of commodity and indirect taxation (with overall lower weight than the direct taxes on the rich and powerful with heavy use of public goods and prime spaces) must of necessity cover the entire spectrum of our vastly differentiated multiple disparities-ridden patterns of social existence and relationships in every single sphere of life. The political and public support-sanction and legitimization based business and public life entities and classes must be held accountable for their decisions on such sets of rarely expounded criteria, criteria which spare the many and soak the few privileged sections. Such a simple but unexceptionable test of progressivity of public decision-making is absolutely missing from the GST proposals.

It is clear ignoring all such social and economic desiderata and mechanical unthinking or rather one-sided thinking based unjust and costly system of GST is sought to be imposed on the general public torn between various unjust differentiation and discriminations, as parts of the overall endemic adverse inclusion. This condition of social existence of the people is prevalent in economic, political, social, cultural spheres. What makes it worse is that even in terms of the laws as they operate at the ground level, whether in the legislatures or law courts or in police stations (which are effectively a law unto themselves), the voice and interests of the common citizens seem to evaporate in thin air.

The entire top-down GST debate has been so debased and has been so orchestrated as to single out and highlight the issues from the partisan angle of the all-powerful corporate-political classes and their unholy alliance by means of and through the network of white-collar crimes forming the difficult to shake base of what is portrayed as India's black political economy Any familiarity with the long-drawn debate and preparations for this one-stroke debasement of the state system has not drawn a real exposure and opposition from any quarter traditionally believed to represent the voice of the weak. Shockingly, many such worthies have been parts of the establishment pushing for and devising the GST, forgetting their conventional lament about the lop-sided powers and responsibilities of the states in the Indian brand of federalism, let alone the interests of the working poor of India.

Some seriously spurious arguments and claims on behalf of the GST lobbies make a strange reading. We are a highly differentiated, non-functionally and unjustly differentiated diverse society and economy. Over two hundred years of commoditization processes in most walks of life have not led us to a well-integrate economy, let alone society and nation. So many attempts at national planning and its so-called progressive core or actually after-thoughts owing to the perverse impact of the GDP centricity as the hegemonic panacea of all our ills have borne little positive pay-off, including the actual life distortions caused by the fiscal policies and spending pattern.

We are in most senses a divided and poorly integrated economy. We have a vast informal-unorganized sector whose primary feature is its spontaneous diversity and variety. It remains the main part of the economy, with over 90 percent share of the workforce it accounts for no more than a half of the GDP. All said and done, no device tried so far has been claimed to have succeeded in producing a well-integrated

Indian economy, even if one ignores the neo-liberal bias of ignoring highly skewed nature of the economy and its inherently desequalizing growth. But lo a and behold with the all-India uniform pattern of indirect tax regime as enunciated and visualized under the GST regime is expected to lead to an integrated economy: one pattern of indirect taxes producing an integrated national economy with a uniform pattern! It seems to be a classic case of wild social imagination, possibly on par with poetic license. Our absolutist empires in the past often had uniform tax systems and the kind of economies they produced is a well-known story.

The fact is that the neo-liberal modes of thought have so pervaded our establishment and the voices of the poor and the marginalized from the policy for a are so sadly missing that it seems to be a matter of a little waiting that the stock markets would surely go in to a celebration mode (sky high share irrespective of corporate economic performance owing to the successful fiscal policy coup) as the GST is enacted into law and collections from the masses start. And as for the companies they have not been taken for a ride by the GST lobbies.

Actually they themselves have been vociferous supporters of GST, and surely not in a mode of self-goal. The moment the GST begins the companies would make their accountants become busy with creative accounting to claim huge sums back from the public exchequer as credits for what they have paid by way of GST at earlier stages of the transactions. State Governments would not be too unhappy as they would get central government compensation for the putative loss of revenue, a gain without the unpleasant decisions to impose taxes. So as the stories end in our folklore, once the GST is in place everybody lives happily thereafter, that is as happily as they have been living for ages! The present day players of the competitive neo-liberal reforms game would parade GST introduction may be in full page advertisements as yet another feather in their cap for successful introduction of major reforms.

8

A Note on GST Bill

Nitish Kashyap

This note takes into account the theoretical underpinnings describing an ideal GST regime and examines the present GST Bill as passed in Lok Sabha and Rajya Sabha. We have done a comparative analysis on theoretical grounds to understand the Bill in its present format with an ideal GST regime and point out the deficiencies, thereby also discounting the celebration attributed to passage of the Bill. We examine critical issues of public finance especially for the developing countries, otherwise neglected in this discourse or sidelined which could have also marked an epoch of political willingness, had those issues been tried to be resolved.

The notion of rules versus discretion is further invoked to understand how gains if any would be difficult to measure by intrusion of powers in hands of states and GST council, which leads to uncertainty about the outcomes regarding tax rate and its structure making any such measurement cloudy. By attributing States and GST council (to be comprised of several members across State and Central government) powers to further decide about its course, creates ex-ante unidentified winners and losers, this fear may lead to sub-optimal outcomes and may lead to adverse outcomes, nevertheless the real test of the policy is time and we keep our fingers crossed to see how it unfolds.

Introduction

With the passage of the modified 122nd Constitutional Amendment Bill on August 8, 2016 in the Lok Sabha, one expects the introduction of goods and services tax in India. With the intent of the present government to rollout GST by

April 1, 2017, the Bill seems to have generated consensus about having a simplified tax regime, more transparency and reduction in incidences of double taxation. It is here that we reflect on this proposed Bill, to understand how we have overtly emphasized the cause of an improvement in our existing tax regime to forego the changes which could have set ideals for modern day public finance for developing countries. We place our arguments discussing the holes in proposed structure and also put forward the arguments which we think are important while discussing public finance in a developing country and are considerably left out in this passage of Goods and Services Tax Bill in India.

Context

We need to have a reference point whereby one can understand the essence behind goods and services tax (GST) becoming operational in India. As the name itself indicates that the way for GST is paved through a Constitutional amendment, in a constitutional democracy, this bill is becoming a reality through our Parliament. The draft of the bill [1] as introduced in 2014 in its 'Statement of Objects and Reasons' reads that "The goods and services tax *shall replace a number of indirect taxes* being levied by the Union and the State Governments and is *intended to remove cascading effect of taxes and provide for a common national market for goods and services*. The proposed Central and State goods and services tax will be levied on all transactions involving supply of goods and services, *except those which are kept out of the purview of the goods and services tax*". Now as pointed in previous paragraph, we first examine if the proposed Bill is self-fulfilling in meeting its objectives and after that we shall examine if it misses largely on crucial facets of Indian public finance which are especially relevant here in discussion. Readers may be told here that we place such a high burden on the legislative in terms of missing largely, on crucial facets from a policy view point considering the fact that this Bill involves a Constitutional amendment which requires special majority in each house of the Parliament following ratification by the State Assemblies. [2]

Criticism

We classify our arguments here in two parts: while one set of arguments would establish how the proposed policy structure is distant from an ideal GST leading to outcomes which are not in tandem with the objectives of the Bill and the second set of arguments would explain more on failures resulting from non-exclusion of certain goods and services.

Is the Proposed GST an Improvement in Terms of Input Tax Credit (ITC) which Firms Can Claim? While the present tax regime with VAT is an improvement in terms of reducing possibility of double taxation, there are still issues with the set-up which remained unsolved and were expected to be taken care of while introducing GST. We point out two such issues here:

- The credit of input VAT could be written off against output VAT. Similarly, the tax credit of input excise/service tax could be set-off against output liability of excise/service tax. In the present set-up, cross-credit of VAT isn't written off against excise and so on.
- Also one can note that State's value added tax is computed on a value including excise duty, and no CENVAT tax benefit is written against it.

Now this denial of due credits imposes an unnecessary cost burden on the assesse and it was thus expected that in GST regime which claims to be an improvement from VAT regime, seamless credit shall be given to firms without curtailment except when goods and/or services in question are availed for personal use. However, one notes that *inter alia*, aforesaid credit would continue to be not available for both goods and services except for inter-State trade. Now this *continuation* of denial perpetuates tax cascading (in fact rate of GST will be higher than the current service tax rate).

Shall Inter-state Trade be Facilitated Better under the GST Regime? This question holds importance considering the objectives of the draft plan which aims for making a *common national market* and it is important that we have neutral tax structure so as not to interfere with production and distribution decisions. Now the provision for an additional tax of 1 percent on inter-State supply of goods accruing to the origin state initially for 2 years, would be distortioning in nature. It would be more severe if the production and distribution of goods and services crosses several states with states up with guns about imposing additional taxes over the uniform prevailing rate. The draft has suggested that it may be extended after those initial 2 years which simply dilutes the possibility of a common national market and sends the possibility into some distant future. One more thing should be pointed here regarding the executing body which decides about such changes i.e. the GST Council.

It comprises of GoI Finance Minister, MoS for Finance and Finance Ministers of State governments or their representatives, while the draft hands over several responsibility and powers to the council, it also rests with the Council the responsibility to solve the disputes which may result from their own decisions. This is alarming seeing the present deadlock in terms of reaching consensus for defining turnover limit for exemption from GST, floor rates, etc. by the technical committee on GST. This concerns us with the fate and strength which GST council can command in future given the multi-party system and rarest of rare possibility of same political flag for all members of the council which would drag the decision-making unnecessarily. This simply does not hint at a common national market in the near future and seem unrealistic as a policy prescription which does not have a timeframe in terms of achieving its goal.

Does it Reduce the Overall Level of Administrative Costs? While we do not have a black and white answer to it considering government and private sector together in picture but one can safely remark that it transfers additional cost burden to corporate houses in general and specifically higher burden to companies engaged in IT services. All firms in general would be required to bring a sea change in their IT practices, for the existing tax structure requires them to maintain a central record of their tax liability and benefits while the proposed plan requires them to maintain state-wise liability and benefits. Apart from this, major challenge remains for the companies engaged in providing IT services, for they would be required to have multiple registrations (as it requires state-specific registrations) based on their client's location which will deepen operating capital cost for these service providers.

Does it Make Markets Distortion-free by Applying Uniform Tax Rates Across Goods and Services? Ideally, it would seem so that uniform taxes do not discriminate between people with different decisions and so affect everyone in same way, leading to efficient outcomes. Though as a policy maker it might sound attractive—one must be on guard given the RNR (revenue neutral rate) predicted by Chief Economic Advisor in Economic Survey which places standard GST rates in the range of 17-18 percent, (contingent upon the fact that exemption base is similar for Centre and States, while this is not the case) while the sub-committee calculates it around 27 percent, both of them are definitely higher than the present 14.5 percent service tax and at least for the short-run would impact the services adversely.

On the top of this, it must be remembered here that the discretionary powers envisaged to the GST Council in terms of awarding exemptions, removing goods/services from consideration, giving short-term benefits, defining turnover limit for considering imposition of GST, they altogether do distort the incentives leading to inefficient outcomes. So, a proposal of equating tax rates on goods and services and still leaving room for discretionary powers in the hands of GST council would actually prove to be a counter current towards achieving distortion free tax structure. In fact while manufacturing would get a boost from such a structure assuming government is able to realize 'Make One India' through creating common national market, the service sector shall receive a setback arising from this sudden differential treatment as compared to earlier and this assumes importance considering an increasing share of services in the GDP.

These set of reasons actually point towards the hole in the basket, whereby we have theoretically and specifically argued about the issues which form part of the proposed structure of the Bill and are problematic in one sense or the other. Adding to the above arguments, one may again extend the cases of GST exemption granted to liquor for human consumption, petroleum products, tobacco products, real estate properties and land deals, health and education, and electricity, to drive home the point that cascading of taxes would still take place—in this sense the reforms are half way towards meeting their objectives.

In a departure from the above line of practice whereby we have focussed on such categories which are excluded or under temporary relief from GST, we now examine the distortionary aspects arising from exemption of these categories and in the end discuss aspects of black economy which remained unshackled in this whole saga of largest tax reforms, post-Independence.

One can understand that leverage granted to petroleum products and electricity goods is again a diversion from self-stated objectives. Besides, these goods being universal intermediate goods, such a provision would lead to cascading effects adversely affecting manufacturing in particular. On the other hand, leaving out health and education again in States' ambit restricts us from achieving social goals of uniformity, which could have prevailed in uniform tax regime. Our main concern is with liquor and real estate included in exempted category, which is a major loss considering streamlining the receipts accruing from two of the most illegally funded business. This last point is seriously alarming, considering the possibility of black money channelled through these business routes and government leaving the taxes to be determined by the States.

In this context, it is good to remember the rule versus discretion debates in economic policy making whereby time and again sticking to 'rules' has been understood effective by policy makers and therefore policy makers who understand the complications of such decision-making arising primarily from political tussle have advocated 'rule' based decision-making. This analogy of rule versus discretion is helpful in highlighting the issue at hand here. As explained earlier, this GST bill which necessitated a Constitutional amendment, we want to emphasize that allowing for discriminatory powers in hands of GST Council or States when we have invested so much in terms of time and energy in getting an amendment passed is something which should be considered as an underachievement.

The point remains that while getting GST passed we as a democracy invested much of our resources in terms of ongoing debates and discussion with stakeholders and the end results still give several powers to GST Council and States, making this whole law making affair being an illusion to create another set of institutions who will take a final call on GST and its details or even each State in turn would decide about levy of rates in their territory. It is in this respect that we consider GST in its diluted form as a heavy cost compared to the cost gone into getting it in its present form.

In light of the above reasoning, we conclude that GST bill is much hyped considering the fact that it is diluted in its present state and we therefore are not much enthusiastic considering the foregone losses which could have been eliminated. More importantly, had real estate and liquor been not exempted and gone to the consideration of States, it would have offered ground resistance to illicit money flowing into these two sectors and would have set a benchmark for making of taxation laws in developing countries. With the passage of Bill in its present form, we consider that opportunity lost and have discussed the skewed disadvantage to services sector which holds more importance for a country like India.

It is not to say that GST when implemented would not lead to any improvement, it may do so but the possibility of such improvement leading to a measurable gain is definitely bleak. With shape of final policy left in hands of GST council and states, there is more uncertainty regarding final figures of tax rates as is reflected by differences in opinions of the office of chief economic advisor and others. We therefore take the GST in its present form with a pinch of salt and would like to see how it unfolds on ground over time.

Endnotes

1. Accessed from Lok Sabha website.
2. Any Constitutional amendment in India needs special procedure for its approval which is long and tiring for any government to get done.

References

"Concept Note on GST", Ministry of Finance, available at: http://dor.gov.in/Gstintro, accessed on March 16, 2016.

Note on GST on Arthpedia website, maintained by Indian Economic Service officers, available at: http://www.arthapedia.in/index.title=Goods_and_Services_Tax.

The Constitution (122nd) Amendment Bill, Legislative Brief, PRS Legislative Research, www.prsindia.org.

Various resources accessed from www.gstindia.com.

Part III:
GST: The International Experience

9

GST in India: Lessons from Canadian Experience

Anjali Agarwal and Amogh Agarwal

Introduction

The introduction of goods and services tax (GST) is a contentious issue in the reform of indirect taxation in India. GST is a value added tax that will replace all indirect taxes levied on goods and services by both Central and State governments. The GST bill conceived in the year 2000 is yet to see the light. More than 160 countries have adopted GST worldwide as the preferred form of tax policy starting from France in 1954. Canada adopted the GST model in 1991 repealing the old Manufacturer's Sales Tax (MST) due to high annual deficits and accumulating debt load. Since, Canada is a federal nation just like India and followed the dual GST concept, it would be a good idea to look into Canada's GST journey and learn few lessons.

Even though the Canadian experience of GST is far from perfect, it represents an uneasy compromise between the political expediency and conceptual elegance. Even though it was met by political turmoil and stiff resistance from the public, its introduction in Canada led to stabilization of tax revenues and increased economic performance. The GST implementation in Canada was simplified by the existence of a single tax collection authority (Federal) and proper infrastructure in terms of management information systems (MIS) and other tax collection mechanisms.

There is a provision for providing tax credits to the economically poorer sections of society and a list of items that are tax exempted. Canada harmonized all the provincial taxes on goods and services by introducing the Harmonized Service Tax (HST) in 1997 after negotiating with three provinces. It continues to bring the remaining states under the ambit of HST by giving special incentives to provinces. The Canadian GST has evolved with time undergoing multiple changes in terms of structure and rates. This shows that if India utilizes this international experience, it will be better prepared to deal with the impending issues.

Goods and services tax is going to be one of the greatest reforms in indirect taxation in modern India, post-Independence. GST is a comprehensive tax levy on the manufacture, sale and consumption of goods and services. It is a consumption based destination tax imposed on all stages of value addition. GST will alter India's federal tax system and unify the country into a single common market. Goods and services will be treated equally and both Centre and States would be able to tax them. GST will subsume all indirect taxes such as excise duty, service tax, value added tax, luxury tax, central sales tax, entry tax and entertainment tax into a single tax payable at the time of consumption.

GST will eliminate the cascading of taxes or 'tax on tax' by introducing a seamless input tax credit ensuring that good quality products made in one part of the country can be conveniently sold in the other parts of the country. Present system results in substantial transaction costs for businesses, as they have to comply with different State tax rules and regulations with different tax rates for same commodity, and it discourages voluntary compliance which leads to revenue leakage (Roy, 2016). GST will improve the ease of doing business as companies will not have to go through the hassle of paying multiple taxes and the seamless access to markets across Indian states will facilitate more efficient production and distribution systems.

GST in India shall have two concurrent components namely: Central GST levied and collected by the Centre and

State GST levied and collected by the States. On inter-State supplies, there shall be levied and collected an integrated GST (IGST) which shall be approximately the total of CGST and SGST. IGST shall also be applicable to import of goods and services and inter-State stock transfers of goods. The exports shall be zero rated under GST giving the price advantage to the exports in international markets. GST's implementation will improve India's image internationally and be welcomed by investors, rating agencies and international experts. Experts believe that the GST will be instrumental in helping the GDP of India to grow by 2 percent and will eventually lead to higher output, more employment opportunities, and economic inclusion.

In a federal country like India, where each State, is sovereign in levying and collecting State taxes, introduction of a blended uniform tax system for all the States is an uphill task. The revenue sharing model between the Centre and States will definitely lead to a financial loss for some of the manufacturing states such as Tamil Nadu. A low GST rate will lead to revenue loss and inflationary impact of high GST rate will impact the entire population—politically suicidal for any government. The tax rate under GST may be anywhere between 18 percent and 27 percent. This value is very high, considering that the global average GST/VAT rate is 16.4 percent; the average rate in Asia-Pacific is 9.88 percent.

Also, in order to appease the States, the final GST model that will be implemented is expected to be weak and far from perfect. For example, several goods have been excluded from the purview of GST like petroleum products, alcohol and electricity. The 1 percent additional tax on inter-State sales was proposed to be collected by the origin State as manufacturing States contend that they, having spent money on putting up infrastructure, would lose out on revenue as GST is essentially a destination tax. These challenges show that it is a long road ahead and it would classify as a true reform only if it meets all our expectations. But the international experience has shown us that it often not the case. GST has been around the globe for more than 60 years and 160+ countries now trust it as the most efficient form of indirect taxation. Hence, it would be a very good idea to take lessons from a country which has successfully implemented the GST and prepare in advance for the problems that may arise.

GST in Canada

Canada is one of those countries which bear a similarity in the political structure to India. Both are federal states and in both the countries, there is a dual structure for indirect taxes, and hence both face similar problems. The Canadian Goods and Services Tax (GST) is a multi-level value-added tax ushered in Canada on January 1, 1991, by Prime Minister Brian Mulroney. Transition of Canada from sales tax to GST increased potential GDP by 24 percent. Analysts estimate that increase in GDP was the result of improved factor productivity and elimination of tax cascading after GST implementation (Venkatraja, 2015).

Prior to the introduction of GST, Canada had a Federal Sales Tax (FST) at manufacturing level, also known as Manufacturer's Sales Tax (MST) which is quite similar to India's Central Excise Duty. It was initially levied upon all sales except retail, to the tune of 1 percent. Over the years, it was increased to 13.5 percent and was seen as a major source of revenue for the federal Government. But it faced downright criticism as it was seen as a system of uncoordinated and high level of taxes covering a very narrow base (one-third of all consumer expenditure) and which had kicked in a cascading effect that compromised the competitiveness of its products in international markets. There were evident ambiguities in the tax structure regarding the distinction of goods and services and the unyielding budget deficit was a major setback to this tax structure.

In view of the complexities of FST, the GST was introduced which covered almost all goods and services at all stages of production and distribution process. The tax is levied at the rate of 7 percent of sales price (Purohit, 2011). Despite its comprehensive scope, GST provides for a few exemptions and zero rating of goods and services. It also provides for tax rebate and low income tax relief.

Some common examples of exempt supplies of property and services are as under:

- Used residential housing.
- Most health, medical, and dental services performed by licensed physicians.
- Child-care services for children 14 years old and younger.
- Legal aid services and educational services.
- Most goods and services provided by charities.
- Certain goods and services provided by non-profit organizations and government.

For tax exempt supplies, the supply is not subject to GST and suppliers do not charge tax on their exempt supplies. Furthermore, input tax credit on inputs is also not allowed.

Some common examples of zero-rated supplies of property and services are as follows:

- Basic groceries such as milk, bread, and vegetables.
- Agricultural products such as grain, raw wool, and dried tobacco leaves.
- Most farm livestock and fishery products such as fish for human consumption.
- Prescription drugs and drug-dispensing fees. Medical devices such as hearing aids.

For *zero-rated* sales, GST is charged by suppliers at a rate of 0 percent so effectively that there is no GST collected. It is eligible to recover any GST paid on purchases used in making the particular supply. This effectively removes the cascading tax from the particular goods and services.

Provincial Sales Taxes

At the sub-national level, all provinces, except Alberta, levy a provincial sales tax (PST). Canada offers three very contrasting models of how sub-national sales taxes might be structured if a federal VAT were imposed:

QST: No role of the Centre, single role of the Province of Quebec.

HST: Single role of the Centre.

PST: Dual role of Centre and State.

Quebec Sales Tax (QST) + Federal Tax (GST)

Because of its strong separatist movement, Quebec often has unique arrangements with the federal government. The Québec Sales Tax (QST) and the federal GST constitute an operational dual VAT system essentially covering most goods and services but not investments. The rates of the two taxes are set independently by the respective governments. The tax bases are also determined independently, although they are essentially the same. From the beginning, both taxes have been collected by a single administration—that of the Quebec province (Table 9.1). Quebec collects GST as well as QST and remits the yield of GST to the federal government (Bird and Smart, 2012).

Table 9.1: QST Historical Rates

Period	QST Rates (percent)
July 1992 to May 1994	8 and 4
May 1994 to December 1997	6.50
January 1998 to December 2010	7.50
January 2011 to December 2011	8.50
January 2012 to December 2012	9.5
January 2013 to Present	9.975

Harmonized Sales Tax (HST)

HST is a consumption based VAT that is currently used in

provinces where the GST and regional PST have been combined into a single value added tax. In 1997, six years after coming into effect, the federal government entered into an agreement with three Atlantic provinces, namely Newfoundland, Nova Scotia and New Brunswick to introduce the Harmonized Sales Tax. HST covers the same goods and services as GST and the new combined rate of HST of 15 percent (i.e. 7 percent federal component and 8 percent provincial component) was significantly lower than the previous combined rate of 19.84 percent in Newfoundland and 18.77 percent in the other two provinces (Purohit, 2011). Export to other provinces was zero rated. HST is administered by the Canada Revenue Agency (CRA) and the State's share is given to the States according to taxable consumption in each province. Inter-State sales are in most cases taxed on a destination basis, with taxes collected by the federal government and allocated to provinces.

From a business point of view, businesses registered for GST are automatically registered for HST. On July 1, 2010 the HST was implemented in the provinces of Ontario and British Columbia despite public outrage. Ontario's HST rate was 13 percent and British Columbia settled for a 12 percent uniform HST rate. On April 1, 2013, British Columbia abandoned the HST and reverted to the GST/PST system through a public referendum on the tax as it was extremely unpopular among the people, due to its perception as a *tax hike*. In 2013, Prince Edward Island opted for HST at a rate of 14 percent.

Retail Sales Tax (RST)

Few provinces continue to operate their RSTs alongside the federal GST. The two taxes are collected by separate administrations (Smart and Bird, 2012). Each province could charge consumers differently and on different items. It is a retail sales tax that is payable when a taxable good, software or service is acquired for personal use or business use, unless a specific exemption applies. Goods refer to tangible personal property as defined in the Provincial Sales Tax Act. Repair and

Maintenance Services along with software are taxable under most provinces. One thing to remember is that it is not a VAT and suffers from the issues of cascading taxes (Table 9.2).

Table 9.2: Tax Rates in Provinces

Year →	1997	1997	2001	2001	2016	2016
Province ↓	Tax rate (%)	Tax type	Tax rate (%)	Tax type	Tax rate (%)	Tax type
PEI	17.7	GST+ PST	10 + 7	PST+ GST	9+ 5	HST
Ontario	15	GST+ PST	8 + 7	PST+ GST	8+ 5	HST
Manitoba	14	GST+ PST	7 + 7	PST+ GST	8+ 5	PST+ GST
British Columbia	14	GST+ PST	7 + 7	PST+ GST	7+ 5	PST+ GST
Saskatchewan	14	GST+ PST	6 + 7	PST+ GST	5+ 5	PST+ GST
Quebec	13.95	GST+ PST	7.5 + 7	QST+ GST	9.97 + 5	QST+ GST
Newfoundland	19.84	GST+ PST	8 + 7	HST	8+ 5	HST
Nova Scotia	18.77	GST+ PST	8 + 7	HST	10+ 5	HST
New Brunswick	18.77	GST+ PST	8 + 7	HST	8 + 5	HST

The initial GST rate of 7 percent stood unchanged for more than 15 years before it was reduced by 1 percentage point in July

1, 2006 and an additional 1 percent reduction effective January 1, 2008, pushing the GST rate to as low as 5 percent. GST is one of the most important consumption taxes in Canada and it accounted for more than two-thirds (69.1 percent) of all federal consumption taxes collected in 2006 (Simonova, 2013). Canada was able to achieve a budget surplus 1998 onwards and so it decided to pass on the dividends to the citizens in the form of GST cuts. Being a consumption tax, even though it disproportionately favours the rich more than the poor, it was seen a welcome change, bringing down household expenses.

Filing of GST Returns

The periods for reporting GST returns are monthly, quarterly or annual, depending on the level of taxable and zero-rated supplies made by the registrant. For a turnover greater than CAD 6 million a year, registrant must file tax returns monthly. Registrants whose turnover is between CAD 15,00,000 and CAD 6 million a year, must file returns quarterly (with an option of filing monthly). Registrants whose turnover does not exceed CAD 15,00,000 must file annually (with an option of filing monthly or quarterly). If the total net tax remittable for the current or preceding year is less than CAD 3,000, quarterly instalments are not required.

Political Turmoil

In 1990, the proposal to introduce GST sparked instant controversy and met a tidal wave of public and provincial opposition for the ruling Conservative Party. The provinces denounced the federal decision to announce GST as unconstitutional, maintaining that a tax on goods and services represented flagrant interference in the field of taxation traditionally reserved for the provinces (Domingue, 2000). They feared giving up major discretionary powers over fiscal policy in a harmonized system. But regardless of its unpopularity, the GST was introduced in 1991 after the standing PM used a special Constitutional provision that allowed him to appoint eight senators on a temporary basis. The resulting election in 1993 was a catastrophe for the conservatives, reducing their position from 169 seats in 1988 to 2 in 1993 in the House of Commons (Sullivan, 2011).

Lessons for India

Even though the Canadian experience of GST is far from perfect, it represents an uneasy compromise between the political expediency and conceptual elegance. In a federal arrangement of government, it easily represents a more practical approach to GST—an approach influenced by various factors to give it its present form. Even though Canada is among the 160 odd nations to have adopted the GST, it is unique in many ways. For example, it is the only nation to reject tax-inclusive pricing (Bird, 2012). Nevertheless, it presents a very good case for India to learn a few lessons from the Canadian GST.

Dual GST Can Work: Canada was able to retain maximum taxation flexibility at all level of governance after negotiation with its provinces. It has a GST at 5 percent at the Federal level and an additional HST at Provincial level of around 8-10 percent for the five participating provinces. Canada substituted the Manufactured Sales Tax (MST) of 13.5 percent levied on producers with GST applicable at 7 percent (now reduced to 5 percent) giving a push to the manufacturing sector especially the exports. The GST also replaced the Federal Telecommunications Tax of 11 percent (Purohit, 2001). Similarly, the Indian government is planning to introduce GST to develop a common Indian market by subsuming all intermediate taxes and reducing the cascading effect of tax on the cost of goods and services. India has also opted for zero rated exports like Canada, to give the Indian exports a competitive advantage in the international market.

Loss Recovery: Like Canadian provinces, the Indian States are also worried about the revenue loss that they would incur because of a consumption based destination VAT, input tax credits and loss of autonomy. In order to harmonize all prevailing taxes, the federal government of Canada undertook to pay $961 million over four years ($349 million in each of the first two years, $175 million in the third year, and $88 million in the fourth year) to the three provinces to offset half of the loss in revenue caused by harmonization (Domingue, 2000). Similarly, in the Indian counterpart of the Bill, the Centre has proposed 100 percent compensation to the States for first three years and 75 percent and 50 percent for the next two years.

Correct Strategy: The harmonization of taxes took place much later from 1997 in Canada after the adoption of GST in 1991. Even though the participating provinces agreed to a Federal GST of 7 percent, they were still continuing with their respective retail sales tax (RST) which wasn't uniform and suffered from the effects of cascading effect of taxes. Gradually, the 3 provinces of New Brunswick, Newfoundland and Nova Scotia accepted the HST and currently 5 states have employed GST. The GST Bill in India requires consent of both houses of the Parliament and 50 percent of States to come into effect. However, the incremental strategy will be difficult in the Indian context as there is no single tax collection authority.

Visibility: Unlike the European Union (or adopted in Australia), retail prices in Canada are quoted before that and the tax is applied at the counter (Purohit, 2001). This was a major source of problem for Canada, as they had to pay additional tax at the cost printed on product. This led to widespread opposition of VAT by the public at large as it was considered an additional tax. In India, It would be a good idea to continue with the maximum retail price (MRP) inclusive of all taxes as it would simplify pricing once all States have uniform taxes.

Exemptions: Since, indirect taxes are the same for every citizen, they are considered regressive as they pinch the poor more than the rich. This calls for a variety of exemptions and differential tax structures. To help maintain revenue neutrality of total taxes on individuals, the federal government issues refundable "GST Credit" of up to $248 per adult and $130 per child to low income people for 2009-10. Provinces offer similar adjustments, such as Newfoundland and Labrador providing a refundable tax credit of up to $40 per adult and $60 for each child.

For one, India will not have a single GST rate and will be implemented with at least three rates in the beginning along with an exempted list. A low tax rate of 12 percent for basic necessities, higher tax rate of 40 percent on luxury goods such as high end cars and a tax rate of 17-18 percent for all other foods and services. But, this kind of a tax system makes the compliance and classification very difficult. Hence, it would be a good idea for India to develop a concomitant support structure, completely delinked from the tax structure by dovetailing it with the existing support schemes of the government like MNREGA to alleviate the burden on poorest sections (Billa, 2011).

Tax Collection Mechanism: Under HST, even though the States decide the rate of taxes, the tax is collected by the federal government and the States are given their share. Similarly, the Federal GST is also administered by the federal government. This ensures that there is a single tax collection agency and the traders/dealers do not have to deal with a new body in every different State. In India, the CGST is administered by the Central Government and the SGST is administered by the State Governments. Having two different bodies for tax collection can complicate the process. From the past practical experience, everyone knows that interpretations, procedures, whims and approach widely differ at both levels. The data of both bodies needs to be synced and any mismatch will hamper the smooth flow of taxes across different jurisdictions. Otherwise, India should look forward to a single body for administering the collection of taxes as it would lead to easier compliance, better manageability of data and fewer complications.

Inflation and Tax Revenues: A general expectation of the public from any tax reform is that it will lead to lower taxes for them. It is also expected that the tax revenues of the government may take a hit, but a wider coverage may offset this temporary phenomenon. In Canada, Introduction of GST did not bring the prices down as the manufacturers did not pass the benefits to the customers (Billa, 2011). Similarly, the federal revenues did not show much increase as it was hyped earlier. The introduction of VAT or change in VAT rates is not inflationary; It might lead to a once and fro all shift in prices, but will not lead to acceleration of prices (Tait, 1988). Hence, owing to international experience, India should not be scared of inflation. The tax revenues are expected to be buoyant as GST is going to result in unification of myriad of indirect taxes and result in increased tax collection due to a larger customer base ultimately leading to economic growth.

Management Information System (MIS): The integrated MIS is a pre-requisite for obtaining all the information from tax returns of individuals and of corporations. The success of GST is highly dependent on availability of technically advanced but user friendly IT infrastructure. The overall system of MIS in Canada is an important pre-requisite and hence, completely integrated. The data capture starts from the time of registration, goes on to payment of tax and processing of returns and draws information for the selection of cases for audit (Purohit, 2001).

The present system in India known as Tax Information Exchange System (TINXSYS) does not appear to be fully operational across all States. The Indian Government has incorporated a company called Goods and Services Tax Network (GSTN), which is a quasi-government company. The GSTN has been incorporated to build, set-up and operationalize the GST common portal. This system will allow taxpayers to register themselves using their permanent account numbers and file tax returns, as well as process payments online. This will also allow collation of data at a central level after which it will be transmitted to the state tax departments.

Conclusion

Even though India and Canada had different motives for introducing the GST, the similarity in their federal system of government and dual GST model ensures that India can learn a lot from the Canadian experience. There is a lot of preparation that needs to done before the introduction of GST in terms of infrastructure, IT network to provide technology backbone, proper division of responsibilities among tax departments and effective redressal of GST grievances. Post-GST implementation of Canada shows that even though the GST was earlier seen as a common enemy, 25 years down the line it has become the mainstay of the Canadian economy. It is expected that the GST will boost the 'Make in India' initiative and ease the regulations for setting up and doing business.

References

"An Insight of GST in India", Vol. 1, The Institute of Cost Accountants of India.

Billa, S. (2011), "Goods and Service Tax (GST): Some Lessons from A Comparison of the Canadian and Indian Models".

Bird, R.M. (2012), "The GST/HST: Creating an Integrated Sales Tax in a Federal Country", *The School of Public Policy*, Volume 5, Issue 12, March.

Bird, R.M. and P.P. Gendron (2007), "The VAT in Developing and Transitional Countries", Cambridge University Press, New York.

Domingue, R. and J. Soucy (2000), "The Goods and Services Tax: 10 Years Later", obtained from Harmonized Sales Tax in Canada, Ontario Edition, prepared by Ontario's Certified General Accountants.

"Harmonized Sales Tax in Canada", Ontario edition, prepared by Ontario's Certified General Accountants, 2009.

Purohit, M.C. (2001), "Structure and Administration of VAT in Canada: Lessons for India", November/December, *VAT Monitor,* 311.

Roy, S. (2016), "Transition to Goods and Services Tax (GST)

Regime: Rationale and Impasse", *The NEHU Journal*, Volume XIV, No. 1, January-June, pp. 51-67.

Simonova, E. and R. Lefebvre (2013), "Is Cutting the GST the Best Approach?", Certified General Accountants Association of Canada.

Smart, M. and R.M. Bird (2012), "VAT in a Federal System: Lessons from Canada, RSM Working Paper No. 2115622, January.

Sullivan, M.A. (2011), "VAT Lessons from Canada", *Tax Analysts.*

Tait, A. (1988), "Value Added Tax: International Practice and Problems", International Monetary Fund, pp. 400-401.

The First Discussion Paper on GST, Empowered Committee, India, 2009.

10

GST in India: An International Comparison

Prabhjote Gill

Introduction

The goods and services tax (GST) has been contended since it was conceived in 2004 by the Kelkar Task Force. Arguments range from the feasibility of the tax reforms to the complexities that it will create, albeit that the entire paradigm rests on the rationale of simplicity and transparency. The spread of the GST system of indirect taxation across the globe indicates an increasing trend, including implementation by 33 of the 34 countries that form the Organization of Economic Cooperation and Development (OECD).

The popularity of this system can be attributed to its preservation of neutrality, widening of the tax base, being a stable source of revenue and ideally being self-enforcing by nature. Each nation has its own reasons and its hurdles to bypass by implementing the reforms of indirect taxation. An analysis of the GST structure that is currently present in some of the major economies of the world with respect to the rate of tax, exemptions, threshold limits, etc., would provide insight into how the current GST structure proposed by the Indian government would hold up with respect to its own shortcomings. This paper takes up examples of the European Union, Canada, New Zealand, and Australia for its comparative review as well as Malaysia, the newest addition to the countries to employ the GST system of taxation.

The procedure of introducing the goods and services tax (GST) is shaping up to be one of the most crucial indirect tax reforms in India. The lack of consensus between the Central government and the State governments, as well as, a few other practical difficulties has resulted in bottlenecks, deadlocks and delays in the implementation process.

The global spread of value added tax (VAT) or GST reinforces the success of the system of indirect taxation over any other form of taxation. With India inching towards a GST regime, there are a set of key expectations with respect to economic development, growth of international trade, stability of prices etc. Further, the taxpayers are expecting the complexity of the current tax system to dilute into something that is simple and uniform and with clarity and transparency.

India, though approaching this new concept with gusto and innovation, can learn a lot from other nations that have already implemented the GST/VAT system within their own economies.

Literature Review

The popularity of the GST and VAT structure of implementing indirect taxes across the globe can be seen by the rapid increase in its implementation in almost 160 countries (OECD, 2014). Each nation has its own motive for implementing the VAT/GST system but the trend can be attributed to the following general characteristics:

1. The VAT/GST system preserves neutrality by taxing the value added by each factor equally.
2. Consumption tax is larger and a more stable source of revenue in comparison to its counterparts.
3. It is potentially self-enforcing in nature thereby reducing the implementation costs in the long-run.

European Union (EU)

The EU implemented VAT throughout Europe in order to replace the cascading multistage turnover tax, as is the current situation in India, in order to facilitate the development of a common market since it made handling cross-border transactions much easier (Council of the European Union, 2006).

The VAT Directive allows for there to be a common structure of VAT but at the same time gives nations, the freedom to set the number and levels of rates that they find suitable, subject to the following constraints (Council of the European Union, 2009):

1. Supply of all goods and services by a taxable person in the course of business within the EU is subject to VAT at a standard rate that may not be below 15 percent, unless specifically exempt.
2. In the case of necessity goods, such as water supplies or pharmaceutical goods, one or two reduced rates may function but they may be no lower than 5 percent.
3. Activities and supplies that are in the public's interest, such as medical care or other services that are associated with welfare, social security, education etc, are exempt from VAT.

Canada

Canada has a federal government, like the one in India, where the system of a federal GST structure was introduced in 1991. Since all provinces continued with the provincial retail sales taxes (PST), there were two levels of levy (Government of Canada, 1985).

The first segment is of the provinces that have harmonized their PST with the GST and hence adhere to what is known as the harmonized sales tax (HST). The HST is a combination of the federal component as well as the provincial component, which is 5 percent and 8 percent respectively. The second segment consists of the remaining provinces where the GST is imposed on taxable goods and services along with the respective PST, which happens only in the three remaining territories of Nanuvut, Province of Alberta and Northwest Territories.

The exceptions to this norm are based on certain policy restraints such as the following:

1. The exports and supplies of goods and services that relate to the basic needs of the population such as drugs, basic groceries, agriculture or transport etc., are zero rated, that is, taxed at zero percent.

2. The supplies of goods and services that adhere to public welfare such as healthcare, education, legal aid etc., are exempted from GST and HST.

New Zealand

New Zealand's tax reforms are important due to the fact that the GST structure that was enacted in 1988 became the international benchmark for how indirect taxes should be designed. When the Fiscal Studies of United Kingdom conducted their evaluation of the European VAT Directives, they used New Zealand's GST model as the basis of their comparison.

The GST Act, 1985 can be applied to most goods and services including many that are considered "difficult to tax", at a rate of 15 percent (Parliamentary Counsel Office, 1985). This Act defined the nature of goods and services as follows:

1. Goods include every type of personal and real property with the exception of actionable claims, money and products transmitted by a non-resident to a resident by means of cable, wire, radio etc., or by other such technical system. Services, thereby, include everything that is not goods or money.
2. The supply of certain goods such as the sale of land, the proceeds from local authorities, sales of going concern (slump sale), etc., are zero rated.
3. The supply of certain goods and services such as donated products and services sold by non-profit organizations, penalty interest, etc., are exempt from the GST.

Australia

The basic rule of the GST structure in Australia is that it is a destination based consumption tax with limited tax base exclusions. When the New Tax System Act, 1999 came into being, it subsumed the federal wholesale sales tax along with selected state and territory taxes with a single tax rate of 10 percent, which is very similar to what India is aiming at doing with its GST system. Similar to other systems, even Australia's GST adheres to certain exceptions (Australian Government, 2015):

1. Certain supplies such as specific food products, most medical services, most educational inputs, religious services, exports, and international transport etc., are zero rated. In Australia they're referred to as GST free.
2. The GST is not applicable on certain supplies such as financial supplies, residential rent, precious metals, and school canteens etc., known as input-taxed supplies or exemptions.

Brazil

Brazil currently has a complex tax system with different levels of taxation and several ancillary obligations leading to unclear legislation and frequent tax litigation. There is no single VAT and hence, the VAT scheme is not comparable. The importance of Brazil for our analysis lies in the fact its complexities and its challenges are similar to what India is currently facing, expressing an even greater need for reforms in the taxation system in order to negate any redundancies and increase the efficiency of the economy (Baker and McKenzie, 2014).

Malaysia

Malaysia's history with respect to its GST is similar to India as the act was first proposed in 2005 but its implementation was repeatedly deferred, that is until April 1, 2015. The GST regime differs quite substantially with the current sales and services tax that Malaysia was adhering to previously (Royal Malaysian Customs Department, 2014).

Objective of the Study

The objective of this study is to analyze India's GST tax system and compare it with countries that have similar tax parameters in order to forecast the impeding challenges and develop strategies to overcome these obstacles is a manner that is feasible, given the constraints faced specifically by a nation like India.

Methodology

To begin with, an indepth study of India's GST tax system is required following which, key concepts that are proposed under the GST structure should be recognized as they will serve as the parameters of comparison with other nations. This information can be easily acquired from the Department of Revenue under the Ministry of Finance with the Government of India.

Next, worldwide tax systems need to be analyzed to determine which countries should be compared with India's GST tax structure. A lot of nations have already applied some sort of VAT or GST but nations like Canada and Brazil are more appropriate for comparison as they have a dual tax system which is similar to what India is trying to apply. Another factor that needs to taken into consideration is the geographical diversity of a nation as well as its economic stature, as both these factors have a strong bearing on how well the tax system will function within a nation and the response of its population. Australia, Brazil and Canada are all nations that are diverse geographically whereas Brazil as well as Malaysia are similar to India with respect to their levels of economic development.

New Zealand and the European Union (EU) should be included in the study to serve as the two extremes that are diverse from the Indian paradigm—where New Zealand is an extremely small nation and the European Union is more economically evolved. This helps to determine what the future may hold with the implementation of an effective GST system and whether or not the ultimate gains attained will be worth the obstacles that need to be overcome.

Analysis

The advantages of moving to a GST structure of taxation

are many, such as reducing the bewildering array of taxes as well as negating the problems that are caused by the extensive cascading. The main issue of levying taxes on things that have already been taxed is the non-transparency of it. It becomes hard to decipher what the effective rate of taxation is on a particular good or service when certain inputs have already been taxed and so had the inputs to those inputs, not to mention the wastage of resources.

This leads to the problem of firms merging their supply chains and functioning in such a way that reduces the level of tax that they would be subjected to but efficiency ends up being the opportunity cost.

The fruits of GST, though, aren't automatic as we can learn via the experiences of other countries.

Bringing Brazil to the forefront, one danger that VAT brings is the excessive differentiation of rates across various goods and services. This, not only adds to the cost of administering the tax but also the compliance cost. It ends up being a very inefficient way of achieving the objectives set out by policymakers. The pressure of setting reduced rates on goods that are largely consumed by the poor segment of the population may be a result of good intentions but the consequences, as such, aren't always intended. The portion of the population that is not so well off may end up spending a large proportion of their income on some item in comparison to the rich but the rich, having greater total income, may as well be spending a larger absolute amount on that same commodity. Hence, the rich, rather than the poor, end up getting the bulk of the benefit.

Another set of issues arises on the treatment of goods and services that are meant to be taxed at higher rates because of the fact that they either cause harm to those who indulge in that particular good or service or may be because that particular good and service is a good revenue raiser. In India's case, the classics are alcohol and tobacco. The main aim of the GST is to raise revenue, not to discourage the consumption of particular items making them less affordable than others. The special taxes that are added thereafter, aim to do both. These taxes should be *specific* so as to charge fixed monetary amounts rather than a percentage of the price. VAT rate and special taxes should be charged together to make sure that the policy has the desired effect.

Now, coming to the EU, there are lessons to be learnt from how inter-State trade is treated. The zero rating of exports between nations, or states as is the case for India, that have minimum or no border controls makes the taxation system vulnerable to fraud. This is the main reason that sub-national jurisdictions have extensive powers in indirect taxation. The IGST concept is an innovative attempt by the Indian government to overcome this hurdle because, so far, no one else has managed to do so.

The roll out of the Malaysian GST hasn't been smooth at all, not only due to deficiencies in the system, but due to the lack of clarity. Lessons to be learnt from Malaysia's experience are that, first of all, the benefits of the new tax system need to be communicated to the public so as to ensure that there isn't any unrest among the masses. Secondly, businesses need to start the implementation process early to be ready for the GST in order to understand the impact that it will have on their business. Clarity need not be 100 percent but the impact of the new tax on their IT systems, processes and other aspects of their business should be assessed.

The Canadian experience shows that it is perfectly possible to operate a dual VAT in a federation given some harmonization and coordination between the centre and the states. Since 1991, Canada has a federal level VAT in the form of FST while the provinces have their own sales tax or VAT. Quebec has own VAT known as the Quebec sales tax (QST). The differences between the QST and GST are almost negligible now. While such differences in the base are not desirable, the GST-QST model shows that these can be accommodated within limits under a dual VAT system. The harmonization of the base and procedures can, and ideally should, be established through a consultative body like the Empowered Committee.

The overall analysis leads to the conclusion that only Canada's HST system has limited disadvantages where, the fiscal autonomy of the States is preserved as well as easier administration is possible by appointing a single agency.

Conclusion

Efficiency should not be viewed only in the narrow economic sense. The trade-off of political efficiency against economic gains would only be short sighted, hence, the Indian government should take its time to implement the GST not only for the sake of making it as efficient as possible.

Centralization of sales is not essential; the Central and State taxes can exist side by side as per the experience of Canada. Given the limitations of the tax department and the experiences of the States in implementing the sales tax, however deficient, every effort should be made to get the best out of the two.

A dual VAT seems to be the most promising alternative with room for the States to have a little bit of freedom with respect to their rates and to a limited extent to their base. Administration at the field level is best left with the States. Audit should be a joint venture but each authority should have the power to institute audit in cases selected by them. Trust and coordination is most essential between the Centre and the States for the smooth implementation of a dual VAT.

References

Council of the European Union (2006), Council Directive 2006/112/EC, November 28, 2006 on the Common System of Value Added Tax, available at: EUR-Lex, http://eur-lex.europa.eu/legal-content/EN/NOT /?uri=celex:32006L0112.

Council of the European Union (2009), Council Directive 2009/132/EC, October 19, 2009, Determining the Scope of

Article 143(b) and (c) of Directive 2006/112/EC as Regards Exemption from Value Added Tax on the Final Importation of Certain Goods, available at: http://eur-lex.europa.eu/legal-content/EN/NOT/?uri=celex:32009L0132.

Government of Canada (1985), "Excise Tax Act, R.S.C., 1985, c.E-15), Government of Canada, available at: http://laws-lois.justice.gc.ca/eng/acts/E-15/page-44.html#h-71.

Parliamentary Council Office (1985), "Goods and Services Act 1985", Inland Revenue Department, available at: `http://www.legislation.govt.nz/act/public/1985/0141/latest/DLM81035.html.

OECD (2014), "Consumption Tax Trends 2014: VAT/GST and Excise Rates, Trends and Policy Issues, OECD Publishing, Paris, available at: http://dx.doi.org/10.1787/ctt-2014-en.

11

Dual and Unified GST: A Comparative Analysis

Pooja Sharma, Ujjwala Gupta and Vanshita Agarwal

India, like many developing countries faces multitude problems like problem of raising enough revenue to meet its growing demand of social and economic infrastructure. Value added tax system has been considered as one of the most significant reforms in the tax structure of developing nations. Though introduction of VAT was a success story in India but there still exist certain drawbacks in the structure of VAT. The introduction of GST at the central level would comprehensively include more goods and services, leading to rise in revenue gain and increased compliance.

This paper focuses on the comparative analysis of two methods of implementing goods and services tax (GST) namely, dual GST system and unified GST system. Dual GST is a type of GST in which both Centre and State governments will levy GST separately. They will have different rates and possibly different commodities and services on which they levy taxes. Unified GST is a single tax applicable throughout the country and which is levied by the Centre and then revenues are shared with the States. Since India is going to follow the GST system, it makes a strong ground to analyse the economies of countries like Brazil, Canada, Singapore and Bangladesh which already have GST for more than a decade. Some of these countries follow dual GST system and some follows unified GST system.

The paper would therefore compare the two methods and derive some useful conclusions from analysing the impact of GST in Brazil, Canada, Singapore and Bangladesh on some crucial macroeconomic variables like fiscal deficit, tax-GDP ratio and foreign trade which play an important role in the performance of an economy.

Introduction

Tax has been an important source of revenue in most of the countries for a long time. It is a financial charge or the levy imposed on the taxpayer (individual or legal entity) by a state or the functional equivalent of state to fund public expenditure like infrastructure, education system and public goods. There are different kinds of taxes and varied tax rates. It is applied to influence the macroeconomic performance of the economy and to modify patterns of consumption and employment within the economy. One of the most important kind of tax is on sales of goods and services which initially were received in the form of value added tax (VAT). But for the past three to four decades, it has been replaced by goods and services tax (GST) which has led to the abolition of other taxes such as octroi, Central sales tax and state sales tax.

Goods and services tax (GST) is a comprehensive tax levy on manufacture, sale and consumption of goods and services. It is collected on value addition in goods and services at each stage of sale or purchase in the supply chain. GST can improve tax collection and boost country's economic development by breaking barriers among states and unify the country into a common national market. There are two types of GST—dual and unified, each having its own characteristics and impact on macroeconomic development. Many of the countries are following either of these two according to their economic and political structure, and as for India, it will follow the dual GST system.

In India, a Central goods and services tax (CGST) and State goods and services tax (SGST) is being levied on all goods and services bearing a few exceptions like petroleum products, alcohol and tobacco. Both GST will be charged on manufacturing cost or value of services rendered which will benefit individuals, as prices will come down. Lower prices will lead to more consumption thereby helping companies and in the long-run benefitting the consumers.

This paper focuses on the impact of both dual and unified GST on macroeconomic variables like fiscal deficit, tax-GDP ratio, inflation and foreign trade in different countries which have already implemented it. Therefore, the paper attempts to draw conclusion regarding the repercussions of implementing GST on the macroeconomic performance of our economy. Although these variables get influenced by many other factors other than taxes but one can visualize the trends in the performance of these countries as the basic idea behind the introduction of GST was to improve the economic performance.

Literature Review

Victor Duarte Lledo (2001) analysed the current tax reforms introduced in the Brazilian tax system. He analysed the short-run and long-run macroeconomic effects of the reform. The reforms introduced, mainly consisted of substituting indirect taxes on corporate which in this paper were proved to be equivalent to symmetric tax on labour and capital income by the new Federal VAT. The paper proves this new structure to have favourable macroeconomic impact both in the short-run and the long-run.

Victor Duarte Lledo (2005) used a dynamic CGE model to analyze macroeconomic impact of replacing turnover and financial transaction taxes in Brazil by consumption taxes. The research concluded that despite an increase in average consumption tax rate in the first year, individuals in the economy experienced lifetime welfare. The paper further rejected the hypothesis that the present fiscal adjustment was a hurdle to implementation of efficient tax system.

Bharati Kiyawat and Shruti Kiyawat (2013) concluded that under the GST system, both Central and State taxes would be collected at the point of sale. Since both Central and State GST would be charged on manufacturing cost and value of services rendered, individuals would benefit in terms of prices coming down. This fall in prices would lead to rise in consumption.

Anushuya, Karam Pal Narwal Junior (2014) analysed the conceptual details of GST using the CGE model. The paper concluded that GST is the most popular tax structure adopted by almost all the countries of the world and CGE is the most effective technique being used to evaluate GST.

Neha Kanojia attempted in her paper to explore the benefits of GST and the current status of GST in the Indian economy. The paper concluded that the current system of indirect taxes is not able to improve competitiveness of the industries. The paper reveals that GST is an improvement over VAT and service tax.

Neha Jain (2015) also concluded that by introducing GST, a significant improvement has been made—it has broadened the base and improved the efficiency of administration.

Tax Structure of India

India has a well developed tax structure with clearly demarcated authority between the Central and State governments and local bodies. But with the changing times, Indian taxation system has undergone tremendous reforms during the last decade. The tax rate has been rationalised and tax laws have been simplified resulting in a better compliance—this rationalisation of tax is still going on in India. The present tax structure in India and the proposed GST structure are as given below.

The present tax structure that India follows is mainly focused on VAT which was introduced as an indirect value added tax in the Indian taxation system on April 1, 2005. VAT—'tax on sale or purchase of good within a state'—is a state subject and central government has been playing the role of a facilitator for successful implementation of VAT. Central government levies taxes on income, custom duty, central excise, and service tax and state levies on VAT and State excise. Although VAT has been successful, yet it has some disadvantages which has forced the government to propose the new GST system.

Proposed GST System

Initially, the GST system was proposed in 2006 with the intention to introduce it by April 1, 2010 but it has been dragged for a decade and was finally (the modified Bill) passed by the Lok Sabha on August 8, 2016 and by the Rajya Sabha on August 3, 2016. GST would ease the burden of trade and industry with respect to the indirect tax system. This tax will be a substitute for all indirect taxes levied by the States and the Central government. Direct taxes like income tax, corporate tax and capital gains tax will not be affected by the GST.

Expected Implications of GST

Abolition of Cascading Effect: Through GST, we can remove the problem of double taxes that are levied on the same product. This double taxation is termed as the cascading effect.

Reduction in Prices: Due to low compliance cost and seamless flow of input credit, manufactures do not to include taxes as a part of their cost of production, which is a very big reason for the reduction in prices.

Increase in Government Revenue: Government wishes to introduce GST at a revenue neutral rate, in which case the revenue will not see a significant increase in a short-run but in long-run, as the central tax collection will increase, there will be an increase in government revenue resulting in reduced fiscal deficit.

Enhanced Competitiveness: Due to the GST, there will be a reduction in the tax burden on companies which will result in low production cost leading to higher output and thus making them domestically and internationally more competitive. As a result of higher output level, there will be an increase in GDP.

Effect on Macroeconomic Variables: GST is a long-run strategy leading to higher employment opportunities and economic boom. It will encourage the start up companies by reducing their tax burden. As GDP increases along with tax, there will be a rise in tax-GDP ratio. These are the expected implications of GST on the Indian economy but to have a more conclusive result, we will study some countries which have already implemented the GST system.

Dual GST System

Canada: Canada is a country following the dual GST system. This system was implemented in 1991 and has undergone lots of changes since then. But initially, the tax structure that Canada followed was the Federal Sales Tax (FST). It applied a 6 percent tax solely on the sales of manufacturers. This undermined the domestic production and in a way promoted imports. Furthermore, it was narrow-based and regressive. It was burdening on a particular section of the society. Because of these drawbacks, Finance Minister Michael Wilson brought GST into play in 1991.

GST replaced the 13.5 percent manufacturing sales tax. As every country has exception, Canada also has exception goods. But the political conditions of Canada were frequently changing as a result of which the economic conditions also changed. Thus, there were many changes in GST after its implementation. In 1997, the harmonized sales tax (HST) replaced the GST. GST led to the fall in prices but not immediately. It also increased the competitiveness of the domestic producers which was initially undermined by the FST. Canada is a country with different provinces having their own tax rates and structure. Some followed only sales tax rate, some levied GST sales tax and some administered both GST and HST. Along with the GST, there was also a tax called PST which was levied in addition to GST on sale of goods. Even with all these changes, the effect of GST was that it alone brought in revenue of about $ 48.511 billion.

Initially, from 1991 till 1994, there was a fall in tax revenue from 14.5 percent to 13.1 percent of GDP, but afterwards from 1994, it increased from 13.1 percent to 14.7

percent. The initial decline in tax revenue (percent of GDP) was because of the political conditions of Canada and also because it took a while to implement the GST throughout the country. After 1997, there was a continuous increase in tax revenue because of implementation of the HST (GST+PST). And as for fiscal deficit, it followed the same trend as tax revenue. Initially, it increased from 5.0 percent to 5.5 percent but after 1993 there was a continuous fall in fiscal deficit and eventually it resulted in a surplus. But GDP followed a bit different trend. As opposed to tax revenue and fiscal deficit, it went on increasing from 1991 to 1994 and after that there were fluctuations without any marked trend.

Brazil: Brazil is one of the few countries which follow dual GST system. It was implemented in 1964. The implementation was done to replace two accumulating taxes that were the IVC and misnamed federal consumption tax. The change in taxes was there to control inflation. The reason behind opting for dual GST system in place of a unified GST was that officials thought that single tax would favour producer states then consumer states. This tax system led to an increase in GDP by 25 percent. The tax system was improved by eliminating federal excises on fuel, electricity, minerals, communications and inter-State transportation, and by incorporating the corresponding tax bases in the ICMS (a VAT which is the main source of revenue of the States). Main changes in taxation system of Brazil were in direct taxes and not in indirect taxes. But as GST was implemented, the contribution of indirect taxes in the tax revenue increased.

Unified GST

Bangladesh: Like any other developing country, Bangladesh faces many problems in raising tax revenue to fund its economic and social development. To improve the economic efficiency, GST was initiated on July 1, 1991 to replace consumption taxes which were narrow based. As every country has its own structure, the same goes for Bangladesh also. Even though they follow a unified GST system, their single tax is very complicated in itself. It was because it included two more taxes which were the turnover tax, a form of sales tax without input credits and an excise type tax known as the 'supplementary duty'. The objectives for introducing GST were to bring greater transparency in taxation system, reducing the cascading effect and to bring greater stability in tax revenues. Here, GST is a consumption type tax levied on consumer goods and not on capital goods.

The tax base for GST in Bangladesh is the difference between value of outputs and value on which input tax has been paid. Initial performance of GST was satisfactory but after sometime, tax collection became stagnant. This was because there were a small number of taxpayers and along with it there was the problem of lack of awareness. Not only this they also faced problems in monitoring the tax collection system. Lack of awareness was there because 48 percent of the population of Bangladesh was in agriculture and private sector that were ignorant of such taxes.

Performance of GST was satisfactory in the initial period but had become stagnant afterwards which was overcome by a substantial contribution to public revenue in later period. This improvement was because of the significant increase in GST registered taxpayers to 598,115 in 2008 from 48,987 in 1992-93 which was approximately 12.2 times more. Percentage share of GST in total tax revenue increased (from 24 percent to 37 percent) while that of custom duty (from 37 percent to 22 percent) and of excise duty (19 percent to 1 percent) decreased during the period 1991-92 to 2006-07. Tax-GDP ratio has been increasing but at a comparatively lower rate than what it should have been. There was a reduction in total revenue collected from GST from 73 percent to 46 percent.

Conclusion

The purpose of this study is to analyse and compare the impact of dual and unified GST on various macroeconomic variables like tax revenue, fiscal deficit, GDP, exports and imports in different countries. This paper concludes that all these countries had implemented GST with the same motive of replacing narrow based taxes and all of them had shown the overall same result regarding their macroeconomic variables despite the difference in their time period of implementation. But there were some changes in their policies which can be attributed to the fact that their social and political structures are different along with the time period in which they implemented these policies. Despite this difference, we observed that effect of GST in countries in initial period is almost the same with little variations. While studying the impact of both dual and unified GST, the paper observes that tax-GDP ratio and GDP growth rate show similar trends while international trade has initially shown a downward trend and then picked up in later years.

References

Ahmad S., V. Ahmad and C. O'Donoghue (2011), "Reforming Indirect Taxation in Pakistan: A Macro-Micro Analysis", *E-journal of Tax Research*, Volume 9 (2), pp. 153-173.

Auriol, E. and M. Wareters (2012), "The Marginal Cost of Public Funds and Tax Reform in Africa", *Journal of Development Economics*, Volume 97(1), pp. 58-72.

Ajakaiye, D.O. (1999), "Macroeconomic Effects of VAT in Nigeria: A Computable General Equilibrium Analysis", AERC Research Paper 92, African Economic Research Consortium, Nairobi.

Andrew, P., M.C. Smith, Ainul Islam and M. Moniruzzaman (2011), "Consumption Tax in Developing Countries: The Case of Bangladesh VAT", Working paper No.82, Wellington New Zealand.

Chadha R., S. Pohit, A.V. Deardorff, and R.M. Stern (1998), "The Impact of Trade and Domestic Policy Reforms in India: A CGE Modelling Approach", The University of Michigan Press.

Lledo, V.D. (2001), "On the Implementation of the Brazilian Indirect Tax Reform", presented in the 2001 meeting of the Latin American Studies Association, Washington D.C., September 6-8, 2001.

Lledo, V.D. (2005), "Tax Systems under Fiscal Adjustment: A Dynamic CGE Analysis of the Brazilian Tax Reform", IMF Working Papers Series, WP/05/142.

Part IV:
GST: Implementation and Implications

12

Impact of GST on Organized Manufacturing Competition

Ashish Kumar Sedai and Aashita Joshi

Introduction

Goods and services tax (GST) is a comprehensive tax levy on manufacture, sale and consumption of goods and services at national level. GST is a tax on goods and services with value addition at each stage having comprehensive and continuous chain of set of benefits from the producer's/service provider's point up to the retailer's level where only the final consumer should bear the tax. There are currently 160 countries of the world that have implemented VAT/GST.

The implementation of GST in India is a significant move in the tax reform of domestic trade taxes in India. It will be replacing the current multiple tax structure (CENVAT/service tax and state VAT taxes). In keeping with the federal structure of India, it is proposed that GST be levied concurrently by the Centre (CGST) and the States (SGST). It is expected that the base and other essential design features would be levied on the basis of the destination principle. Thus, inter-State supplies within India would attract an Integrated GST (aggregate of CGST and the SGST of the destination State).

On the contrary, we have the manufacturing sector lingering with dismal growth performance and even registering 0 percent growth in the recent past. It is immediate to understand what will be the impact of tax reforms to the most ambiguously taxed sector of the economy. It is also interesting to see how a reform in tax can change the structure of manufacturing competition in the Indian Industry. To understand competition in the market, we should look around us. Can you say that around us we see monotony in the products we consume. Manufacturing is growing slow and the market structure is moving towards an oligopoly in almost all manufacturing, especially the chemical and drugs industry.

The paper aims at understanding the implications of implementation of goods and services tax on the manufacturing sector of the country. The manufacturing sector is a thriving sector of the economy and any change in the taxation system will have a major impact on the sector. Hence, the objective of the paper is to explore the positive and negative impacts of the GST on the manufacturing sector and provide specific changes in the different types of taxes that are vital for the sector.

Analysis

The study is a panel data analysis of the structural characteristics of the manufacturing sector. Market concentration indices used are Hirrschman Herfindahl Index (HHI) and the Concentration Ratio Four (CR4). The following figure shows the trends in the manufacturing sector in India. The findings strongly support the positive effects to be brought by a change in the taxation system and also show a need to evolve the system to best complement the growing manufacturing sector of the country. Trends in manufacturing sector can be seen in Figure 12.1.

There has been a mismatch in the rate of growth of firms across the time period since 1960. The maximum increase that has occurred in the number of firms entering the industry has been during the two decades from 1980-2000, more specifically during the decade 1990-2000. An increasing number of firms entering the industry would mean that the level of competitiveness in the industry has been on the rise overtime (Mishra, 2011).

On the contrary, the decline in the number of firms entering the industry post-1999 has been drastic, more than two hundred percent for all the industries combined. The reasons for such decline in the number of firms entering the industry can be explained by:

- Reaping the benefits of early reforms completely.
- Saturation of markets.

Figure 12.1: Trends in the Manufacturing Sector

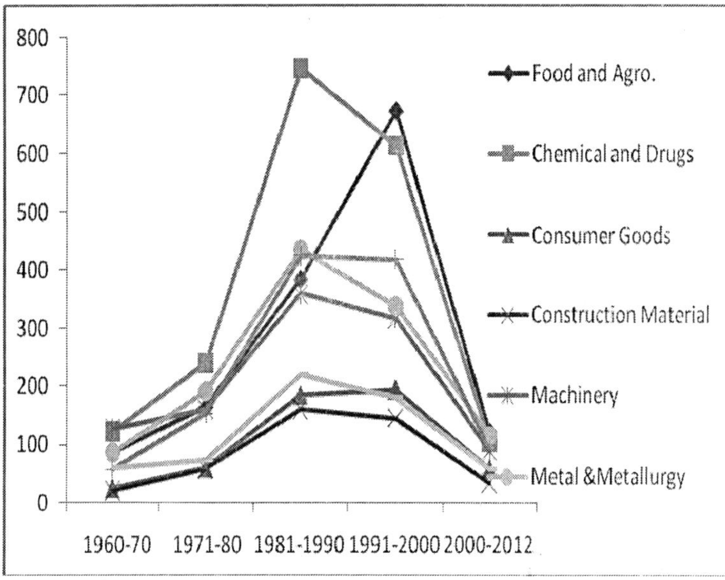

Source: CMIE.

These arguments seem to lose ground when we see the reforms process as a perennial activity; giving tax incentives, easy clearance, special economic zones to facilitate industrial activity as the main agenda of economic growth in India overtime. Saturation of market hypothesis seems to be a far cry as far as the market for manufacturing goods in India is concerned. This can be seen by the level of investment in Indian manufacturing both domestically and via foreign investment. Manufacturing sector in India has been the second highest collector of foreign investment during the period 2000-2010 and the country with highest net FDI in 2015. With this rationale of growing market concentration in mind, the research problem has been framed.

There has been a rapid increase in the number of firms after economic reforms and a decline in the number of firms since 2000. Manufacturing competition has intensified amongst major players and, there seems to be a decline of small and marginal firms.

The GST will distribute the taxation burden, remove cascading effects and hence bring down prices for the final consumer. This would have several implications on the market share of industries. By reducing the average cost by firms (especially large scale), firms' GST would partially aid in monopolizing the industries.

The price competitiveness of the unorganized entities is likely to deteriorate, resulting in narrowing of the price differentials. This is likely to lead to accelerated top line growth and also increase in market share of the organized players. Companies like Bata India (footwear), Kajaria Ceramics, Somany Ceramics (tiles), Mayur Uniquoters (artificial leather), Finolex Industries (pipes), Pidilite (adhesive), etc. may benefit from unorganized players losing the price differential benefits post-GST.

How Will Manufacturing Benefit from GST?

It is interesting to note how and which firms would benefit from the simplification of the taxation system especially given the fact that the burden of GST is ultimately to be borne by the customer. Under the existing system, a firm has to undergo the incumbent/orthodox multiple and hidden taxes which hinders the inception and expansion of firms. There are nearly 20 odd taxes that are levied on the manufacturing sector. Four of these taxes are discussed in detail below along with the changes that would come in these taxes once GST is implemented.

In addition to the IGST, an additional tax of up to 1 percent has been proposed to be levied by the Centre on the supply of goods. The revenue from this tax is to be assigned to the origin States. This tax is proposed to be levied for initial two years or such longer period as recommended by the GST Council.

The need for GST arose from the various shortcomings of the current tax structure in India. This shift to an integrated and simplified tax structure is not only desirable but also imperative in the emerging manufacturing environment. There are several drawbacks present in the current tax system. The current system in an amalgamation of multiple rates, irrational structure of levies and existence of several exemptions. The general rates of States' VAT include 4-5 percent on goods of basic necessity, such as food and the export of goods from India; 1 percent on gold and silver ornaments; 5 percent on declared goods and machinery; 12.5 percent to 15 percent on all other goods; and 20 percent or more on fuel, diesel, cigarettes, and lottery tickets.

This seems absurd as the basic necessity goods are taxed at a rate high than the precious metals (which are luxury goods). This clearly shows the complexity of the tax regime. The problem of cascading is a severe one as it leads to double taxation on goods and hence impacting the final price of the goods. The increased cost of production puts the Indian suppliers at a comparative disadvantage in the international market. Even in the domestic market, a bias is created towards the imports of competitive foreign goods as they do not carry the hidden burden of input taxes whereas the domestic manufactured goods do. All these disadvantages of the current tax regime are effectively tackled by the GST system.

Excise Duty (CENVAT)

Central excise duty is an indirect tax levied on those goods which are manufactured in India and are meant for home consumption. The taxable event is 'manufacture' and the liability of Central excise duty arises as soon as the goods are manufactured. It is a tax on manufacturing, which is paid by a manufacturer, who passes its incidence on to the customers.

Broadly, the following types of duties are levied by the Central Government on goods manufactured in India:

1. Basic excise duty.
2. Education cess and secondary and higher education cess on excise duty.
3. National calamity contingent duty.
4. Duties under other Acts.
5. Specified duty.
6. Duty based on the production capacity.

The CENVAT is levied on the goods manufactured in India. An unavoidable difficulty arises in terms of classification of manufacturing activities and its value addition in the production.

Under the GST system of taxation, excise duty will be subsumed under the CGST (Central goods and service tax). A dual system of tax will be followed where tax is collected independently by the States and the Central government. Central excise duty, additional excise duty, services tax and additional duty of customs would be subsumed within the GST. The common base for GST would enable the manufacturers to pay one tax instead of about 16 taxes being currently paid. The uniformity in taxation would lead to better compliance and more transparency.

Export Tax

Taxes on exports are all levies on goods being transported out of the country or services being delivered to non-residents by residents.

Customs duty is applicable on the goods exported from the country. The current export tariffs in India as per the EXIM Policy of India covers exports tariff rates for different goods and services. The tax levied on the export of goods makes the Indian products less competitive in the foreign markets. Basic necessity item like sugar is taxed at 20 percent and basmati rice at ₹ 12,000 per tonne whereas metals like iron ores face a tax rate of 40 percent. The export duty most definitely adds a huge cost to exporting. Thus, a hidden burden of taxes is reflected in the prices of Indian goods competing in foreign markets. Equal in quality yet lacking behind due to prices, a favourable change in the tax system can boost the exports from India.

Under the GST taxation system, tax on export would be zero-rated. The destination based tax system provides for the exports to be tax free. This can cause a huge difference in the competitiveness of Indian products in the foreign markets. This can prove to be good for the Indian economy in the long-run.

Central Sales Tax (CST)

CST is a tax on the sale of goods levied by the Central government of India. CST is applicable only in the case of inter-State sale. Inter-State sale is when a sale or purchase constitutes movement of good from one State to another. CST is payable in the State where the goods are sold and the movement commences. The tax collected is retained by the State that collects the tax.

Under the GST system, the existing CST will be discontinued. Instead, a new statute known as IGST will come into place. It will empower the GC to levy and collect the tax on the inter-State transfer of the GS. The scope of IGST model is that Centre would levy IGST which would be CGST plus SGST on all inter-State transactions of taxable goods and services with appropriate provision for consignment or stock transfer of goods and services.

The change in tax regime will bring about many positive changes for the manufacturers. There will be a common market in the absence of CST and entry tax. At present, goods are being sold mostly within the State in order to avoid paying the CST which is not credited at the stage of manufacture or in course of trading.

Good quality products being manufactured in one part of the country will find more market in the farthest part of the country because there will be no CST and no entry tax. The abolition of entry tax will be a great boon for the movement of goods by road transport, thus, reducing the transportation time of the manufactured products.

Conclusion

The change in taxation system, a move towards GST is a positive indicator for the manufacturing sector. The overall growth of the sector can be significantly affected by the introduction of the GST system.

The paper concludes by emphasising on some benefits of the GST system. The prices of commodities is likely to witness a significant drop due to presence of full and seamless credit, since manufacturers or traders would not have to include taxes as a part of their cost of production. The change in taxation system would increase the government revenues also. Even though this might appear to be vague however, even at the time of introduction of VAT, the public revenues actually went up instead of falling because many people resorted to paying taxes rather than evading the same.

An efficient movement of goods and services throughout the country and better competitiveness of domestically produced goods internationally is unquestionably a desirable boon for the economy. Hence, GST is an unavoidable upgrade required in India's tax regime which would indefinitely provide more benefits to the economy than obstacles— manufacturing sector being one of its greatest benefits recipient.

References

Bain, J.S. (1956), "Barriers to New Competition: Their Character and Consequences in Manufacturing Industries", Harvard University Press, Cambridge, M.A.

Baltagi, B., and S. Song, S. (n.d.), "Unbalanced Panel Data: A Survey", *Statistical Papers,* pp. 493-523.

Barthwal, R. (1984), "Industrial Economics: An Introductory Textbook", Chapter 5, pp. 89-93, New Delhi: Wiley Eastern.

Belman, D., and J. Heywood (n.d.), "Market Structure and Worker Quality", *The Journal of Industrial Economics,* pp. 155-159.

Bhattacharya, K., and A. Das (2003), "Dynamics of Market Structure and Competitiveness of the Banking Sector in India and its Impact on Output and Prices of Banking Services", Reserve

Bank of India Occasional Papers, Volume 24.

Mishra, P. (2011), "Market Concentration and Competitiveness", *Indian Development Review.*

13

GST and the Present System of Indirect Taxes: A Comparison

Saurabh Jain and Priti Jain

Goods and services tax (GST) is a destination based consumption tax which is proposed to be levied on each stage of value addition in the supply chain. GST is considered to be the largest reform in the Indian tax laws in the post-independence era. At present, in India, we have around 15-20 major indirect taxes which are being levied on various transactions of sale of goods and rendering of services. This multiplicity of indirect taxes leads to vast disadvantages in the form of cascading effect of taxes i.e., tax being levied on tax, when multiple taxes are levied on a single transaction and such taxes form part of cost as it flows through the value chain. GST as proposed shall subsume various indirect taxes and with seamless input-tax credit being its backbone, it is going to be revolutionary in mitigating the cascading effect of taxes.

Secondly, the different indirect taxes are governed by their respective statutes, each statute has its own definitions and interpretations with respect to various terms, which often results in huge litigations particularly due to interpretational issues, e.g. with respect to computer software, there is an ongoing debate whether the same should be treated as goods or service—this identical issue is involved in many cases pending in various tribunals and courts of law. GST as proposed shall be one comprehensive law instead of various indirect tax laws which are presently in force and hence GST shall put an end to the plethora of cumbersome litigation on account of such interpretational and other issues.

Thirdly, in the present sales tax and value added taxes, numerous exemptions are available for different transactions like stock-transfers etc. which leads to manipulation of transactions by business houses in order to avoid taxes. Such tax avoidance mechanisms involve huge non-value added costs to the business houses and loss of revenue to the Government. GST as proposed shall do away with such loopholes and therefore, save such unproductive costs of the business houses and minimize revenue loss for the Government.

In view of the above background, various aspects of the proposed GST regime have been discussed in detail in the following order:

1. Salient features of the proposed GST.
2. Broad distinction between the present system of indirect taxation and proposed GST law.
3. Advantages of the proposed GST to the taxpayers.
4. Advantages of the proposed GST to the exchequer and government.
5. Expectations from the Central and State governments.
6. Implications of GST for the Indian economy.
7. Impact of GST on consumers and businessmen.
8. Impact of GST on inflation and GDP.
9. Impact of GST on 'Make-in-India'.

Salient Features of the Proposed GST

1. GST is a tax on supply of goods and services other than on alcohol for human consumption.
2. GST is a destination based taxation.
3. GST shall apply to all stages of the value chain.
4. GST shall apply to all taxable supplies of goods or services (as against manufacture, sale or provision of service) made for a consideration except exempted goods or services, goods or services outside the purview of GST and transactions below threshold limits.
5. GST in India shall have two concurrent components namely: (a) Central GST levied and collected by the

Centre and (b) State GST levied and collected by the States.

6. On inter-State supplies, there shall be levied and collected, an integrated GST which shall be approximately the total of CGST and SGST.
7. IGST shall also be applicable to import of goods and services and inter-State stock transfers of goods.
8. Export of goods and services shall be zero rated under the proposed GST.
9. All goods or services are likely to be covered under the GST except:

- Alcohol for human consumption—which is liable to State excise plus VAT.
- Electricity—which is liable to electricity duty.
- Real estate—stamp duty plus property taxes.
- Petroleum products—this shall be brought under GST from the date to be notified on recommendation of the GST Council.

Distinction between the Present System of Indirect Taxation and the Proposed GST Law

Structural Difference: Under the present system of indirect taxation, there are two separate VAT systems operating simultaneously at two levels i.e., Centre and State. The tax paid under one system is not available as a set-off against the other i.e. input tax credit is not available across the taxes levied by the Centre and the States. Further, tax on services i.e. service tax is levied under a separate legislation by the Centre and the States have not been given the right to tax the services.

Under the proposed GST regime, a dual tax with both Central GST (CGST) and State GST (SGST) shall be levied on all taxable supplies. All the goods and services, barring a few exceptions, shall be brought under the GST base and there shall be no distinction between goods and services for the purpose of tax with a common legislation applicable to both. It shall allow seamless tax credit across various duties and taxes i.e. excise duty, service tax and value-added tax.

Place of Taxation: Under the present system, tax shall be levied and collected by the originating State in case of goods and by the Centre in case of rendering of services.

Under the proposed GST regime, tax on all taxable supplies (of goods and services) shall be shared between the consuming or destination State and the Centre, except an additional tax of 1 percent which shall be given to the originating State.

Tax on Imports into India: Presently, goods are taxed to customs duty which comprises basic customs duty, CVD and SAD. Under the GST, the basic customs duty shall remain the same; however, CVD and SAD shall be subsumed into GST.

Tax on Inter-State Transfer of Goods to Branch/Depot or Agent: Presently, such inter-State transfers are exempt against Form-F prescribed under the Central sales tax laws. Under GST, all such inter-State transfer of goods shall be taxable.

Cascading Effect: The present system of indirect taxation allows tax credit between excise duty and service tax but not with VAT. The proposed GST shall allow seamless tax credit amongst excise duty, service tax and value added tax.

Cost Burden on Consumers: Under the present system, due to presence of cascading effect, certain taxes become part of the cost which puts undesirable burden on the consumers. As GST mechanism removes such effect by providing seamless input-tax credit, cost burden shall be reduced.

Exemptions: Under the present system, there exist various exemptions by way of excise free zone or various exemptions under VAT laws. Under the GST, all such exemptions may go in a phased manner.

Compliance: Under the present system, tax compliance is complex because of multiplicity of laws and their numerous provisions. Under the GST, tax compliance would be easier as only one law subsuming other taxes shall be required to be followed.

Concurrent Powers of the Centre and the States: At present, there is no such power to both Centre and States on same subject tax matter. Under the proposed GST law, both Centre and States would be vested with the power to make laws on GST by virtue of the proposed Article 246A of the Constitution.

Advantages of the Proposed GST for the Taxpayers

Reduction in Multiplicity of Taxes: Under the GST regime, businesses shall be required to pay a single tax i.e. GST on each stage of value addition vis-à-vis paying a number of different taxes with respect to same transaction in the present indirect tax structure.

Mitigation of Cascading/Double Taxation: Under the present system of taxation, there are various taxes which become part of cost of goods and services as they flow through the value chain, due to non-availability of seamless input-tax credit. This results in cascading effect or double taxation. Under the GST regime, majority of such cascading or double taxation shall be mitigated except for 1 percent additional tax.

Seamless Input Tax Credit: The GST shall facilitate seamless credit across the entire supply chain and across all States under a common tax base. The present structure allows limited inter-levy credits between excise duty (tax on manufacture) and service tax. Advent of GST shall rationalize tax content in product price, enhance the ability of companies to compete globally and possibly trickle down to benefit the ultimate consumer.

Creation of Common National Market: Presently, due to existence of taxes where no input tax credit can be claimed such as CST and entry tax, goods are preferred to be sold within the State in order to avoid such taxes. With the advent of a unified tax i.e. GST having seamless input tax credit mechanism, good quality products manufactured in one part of the country would be conveniently sold in the other parts of the country. This shall even have appreciable favourable effect on competition in India and thereby result in creation of a common national market for quality goods.

Elimination of Various Unproductive and Non-value Adding Costs Incurred during Transportation of Goods: Presently, in order to pay the entry tax, the goods carriage vehicles are required to stand in long queues at the borders of States. This leads to incurring of various unproductive and non-value adding costs such as fuel costs, idle time costs of both the carriage drivers and workers at factory site awaiting the arrival of raw material etc. The delay caused in transportation of goods due to entry tax barriers hampers the entire production and supply chain resulting in huge losses in a number of ways. GST shall do away with majority of such losses by subsuming the entry tax.

Common Exemptions between the Centre and the States: Presently, different exemptions are being offered by the Centre and the States under various indirect tax laws which lead to difference in pricing of goods thereof. Under the GST regime, exemptions will be common between the Centre and the States which shall make the rates of duty same all over India.

No Distinction between Goods and Services: In many cases, like computer software, dispute arises due to distinction in their treatment as goods or services. These disputes shall come to an end under the GST regime, where both goods and services shall be treated alike and shall be termed as a 'taxable supply'.

Lesser Classification Controversies: Presently, classification controversies are in abundance since there are so many rates of duty. This problem shall also go away as there would be minimal exemptions under GST.

Benefits of GST for the Centre and the States: GST shall promote enhanced exports, create more employment opportunities and boost growth. It will divide the burden of tax between the manufacturing and the services. This shall result in an equitable distribution of tax revenues between the Centre and the States.

Advantages of GST to the Exchequer and the Government

Simpler Tax System to Administer: Present structure of indirect taxation is quite complex in its administration due to a number of legislations governing different types of taxes. The proposed GST regime shall do away with such administrative difficulties and result in a simpler tax system to administer.

Broadening of the Tax Base: There will be a number of benefits for the taxpayers which shall result in broadening of tax base under the GST regime. Further, there shall be lower threshold exemptions under the GST which will consequently result in broadening of assessee base and hence higher revenue for the government.

Improved Compliance and Revenue Collections: The availability of seamless input tax credit coupled with simpler administration of the system of taxation under GST shall result in improved compliance and revenue collections.

Curb on Black Money: Prevailing system of without-invoice transactions results in generation of unaccounted income as it escapes tax nets of both direct and indirect taxes. GST would encourage invoicing and consequently it shall be instrumental in curbing the menace of black money.

Expectations from Central and State Government

Centre-State Interaction: Considering the federal nature of our country and Centre-State relationships, Central Government should be prepared to pass more powers of taxation to the States and share more revenue with the States, in order to make GST a success.

Constitutional Amendments: Under the scheme of our Constitution, no tax can be levied without the authority of law. Power to levy tax on goods and services are vested with both Central Government and the State Governments under Article 246 and List-I and List-II of the VII Schedule of the Constitution of India. Neither the Central Government nor the

State Government can usurp the powers of others without amending several provisions of the Constitution.

Stability of GST Act and Rates: As recommended by Dr. Kelkar, there should be an agreement between the Central Government and all State Governments that there should not be any change in the GST Act or rates without concurrence of both Central and State Governments. Only this can lead to stability of the GST Act and will give global reputation to the Indian continent. Such gearing up for GST by the two tiers of Government is the industries' expectation because it will facilitate smooth introduction and operation of GST.

Re-engineering of Central and State Employees: There should be a thorough re-engineering of the department of GST at Central level as well as the State level. This is very much required to clearly define, understand and administer functions in such a way that the responsibility, accountability and authority of each tax department at the Central and State level is clearly understood.

Single Authority to Deal With: As it is known that the number of officials at the Centre is less as compared to State level officials, it is expected that Central officials be assigned special task to monitor the operations of large dealers (who have pan-India operations) under CGST and SGST. The day to day operations related to registration, payment of tax and submission of returns for all the dealers (irrespective of their size) should be assigned to the States. The assessees with specific turnover, say up to ₹ 500 crore and the assessees whose operations are limited to one State only should be assessed by the State Department for both CGST and SGST. In general, the idea is that assesses should interact with a single tax authority only. Presently, under the recommendation of Joint Working Group, CGST will be monitored by the Central Government and SGST will be monitored by the State Government. It means that assesses will have to deal with two authorities which may be unacceptable by all dealers. Going by the past experience, everyone knows that interpretations, procedures, whims and approach widely differ at both the levels. If this happens, then instead of helping, GST will create more harassment and nuisance.

Verification Agency: Cross verification of documents should be strengthened under the GST to avoid evasion and wrong claims.

MIS Amongst Different Government Departments: MIS has to be an integrated activity of the CGST and SGST offices as well as other Government Departments.

Creation of IT Infrastructure: The government has created a company called GST Network (GSTN) to provide the technology backbone to introduce GST and connect the databases of States and the Centre. In this regard, a contract for a period of 5 years has already been awarded to Infosys by GSTN. The information technology (IT) system will allow taxpayers to register themselves using their permanent account numbers and file tax returns, as well as process payments online. This will also allow collation of data at a central level after which it will be transmitted to the State tax departments, thereby preventing tax evasion and widening the tax base to include more traders.

Implications of GST for the Indian Economy

Hitherto, introduction of value added tax (VAT) at the State level and CENVAT at the Central level are considered to be the largest indirect tax reforms in the country and GST is considered to be most reformist step towards making India a unified market. The biggest advantage of GST is economic unification of India. It has potential to end the long standing distortions arising out of the differential treatment of the manufacturing and service sectors.

Further, it would also improve tax compliance by making it easier for businesses to return files, pay taxes and get refunds. For importers, the input tax credit would be available for countervailing duty of customs (CVD) and additional customs duty (ACD) and thus would help them. GST would substantially enhance the competitive edge of both the manufacturing and services industry by removing the disability that domestic producers suffer from.

Impact of GST on Consumers and Businessmen

The several types of taxes that currently exist such as excise, octroi, sales tax, service tax, turnover tax etc. would come under the GST umbrella. Since this would eliminate double taxation, it is expected to result into fall of prices, thereby relieving the consumers. This is mainly because the GST provides tax credit at every stage of taxation from manufacturing to consumption. Currently, margin is added at every stage and tax is paid on the amount including margins. These taxes on profit and taxes on tax add to the cost of goods and services whose burden is to be borne by the final consumer. GST would provide a continuous chain of set-off from the producer's point to the retailer's point and would consequently result in fall in prices. The chain of set-offs would also result in better tax compliance by industry, trade and businessmen. For businesses, GST would make life easy because of easier compliance (due to absence of multiple taxes) and easier return filing, tax payment and refund process due to robust IT infrastructure, which is considered to be the backbone of its successful implementation.

Impact of GST on Inflation and GDP

The GST with its uniform taxation structure can be one of the most important steps towards achieving the task of inflation management and GDP growth. The current indirect tax regime suffers from significant cascading which leads to higher cost of goods and services consumed in the country. There are also numerous examples where the taxpayers or consumers have to pay both the Centre and State, taxes on a single sale which adds to increased tax costs for businesses and consumers. Such increased costs add to the inflationary pressure in the economy. In the GST regime, a free flow of credits across transactions decrease the tax cost for businesses. Given that both Centre and State taxes would be levied simultaneously on all supplies, the issue relating to dual taxation on certain products would also come to rest. The decrease in tax costs would boost the exports in the country. The reduction of costs in India would make our products more competitive in the international market thereby not only increasing the GDP of the country but also inflow of foreign currency. There are also estimates that GST can add up to 2 percent to the GDP.

Impact of GST on 'Make-in-India'

The 'Make in India' campaign proposes to make India a world class manufacturing hub. The tax reforms through GST will play a crucial role to attract large scale investment. The proposed goods and service tax (GST) promises a progressive tax system which avoids tax cascades and helps establish India as a true common market. GST will reduce the cost of production and allows the hassle free supply of goods. As per a report of the World Bank Group on Ease of Doing Business and Paying Taxes, India ranks at 130th and 157th place among 189 countries of the world—this ranking is expected to improve substantially with the implementation of the GST.

In view of the foregoing discussion, it can be concluded that the proposed GST which is a comprehensive system of indirect taxation would prove to be the largest tax reform as well as a business reform in India.

References

First Discussion Paper on Goods and Services Tax in India, The Empowered Committee of State Finance Ministers New Delhi, November 10, 2009.

Kelkar, Vijay (2012), "Report of the Committee on Roadmap for Fiscal Consolidation", Ministry of Finance, Government of India.

Poddar, Satya and Ehtisham Ahmad (2009), "GST Reforms and Intergovernmental Consideration in India", Working Paper No.1/2009-DEA.

Statement of Objects and Reasons appended to The Constitution, (One Hundred and Twenty-second Amendment) Bill, 2014.

14

Implications of GST: A Critical Analysis

Sanjiv Ranjan

India is having a differential tax system and so the system of indirect taxes such as excise duty, customs duty, sales tax, service tax etc. which are taxed by the Centre and the States respectively. History had witnessed reformation in the taxation system to make it simple, transparent and accountable like in the case of VAT and service tax. One such new attempt is the latest debate for GST (goods and services tax). GST is a consolidated and integrated taxation system with the aim of subsuming every other indirect tax into a single taxation system and is called as VAT because at every stage, tax is being paid on the value added to the goods and services. It has its own pros and cons and is stuck in quagmire just like bullock cart stuck in mud (Govind, M.R., 2011). Apart from an increased tax base, simplified taxation policy and redistributive taxation policy between manufacturing and service sector, it poses certain challenges for the States' fiscal autonomy like its cascading effects and sharing of revenues between the Sun belt [1] region and rust belt [2] regions per se.

This article will aptly study the GST through critical perspectives highlighting both sides i.e. grey areas and greener one and then will direct some customization needed in the GST structure as a policy. I will be mentioning the economic and political implications of the GST and then moving towards the restructuring process.

Introduction

The system of indirect tax in India had witnessed reformation with GST as one such major reforms which was mooted by the then union minister Shri P. Chidambaram in 2006-07. However, in the year 2000, for the first time, the idea of initiating the GST was made by the then Atal Bihari Vajpayee Government with formation of Empowered Committee headed by Asim Dasgupta (finance minister of West Bengal). The year 2011 again witnessed push from the UPA government with introduction of Constitutional amendment bill to facilitate GST but was rejected by many states (Phukan, 2015). The recommendation of Empowered Committee which rolls out its first discussion paper in 2009 presented some salient features of the GST.

However, this did not go well with the States and so attracted a debate. The GST is a tax that a consumer has to pay as the final tax every time he/she buys goods or services. It is levied on the VAT at every stage of production so it is sometimes called as VAT (Bureau, 2009). It seeks to re-institutionalize and integrate the current system of indirect taxes into a consolidated one, procurement of which will be then divided among States in a prescribed ratio. Thus, GST is a consolidated tax base system on a uniform rate for both goods and services and is payable at the final point of consumption. At each stage of sale or purchase in the supply chain, this tax is collected on value added to goods and services, through a tax credit mechanism (Phukan, 2015).

The GST reform is going to broaden the tax base, decrease distortions, enhance export competitiveness and ensure a seamless national market by removing inter-State trade barriers. The uniqueness of this new policy can be understood after comparing the CENVAT (levied on goods production, but value added in next stage is not included in the base) and the authority given to the state to tax on services through it (Govind, R., 2014). Presently, GST is 3 tier system with CGST (central goods and service tax) levied by the Centre, SGST (state goods and services tax) levied by the States and the IGST (integrated goods and services tax) to be levied on inter-State supply of goods and services which will be collected by the Centre with no cross utilization of CGST and SGST credit.

The policy will be functioning on the principle of *destination based* that means exports will be *zero-rated* while imports will be subjected to GST.

The salient features of GST are discussed below:

1. The power to make laws in respect of supplies in the course of inter-State trade or commerce will be vested only with the Union government. States will have the right to levy GST on intra-State transactions including on services.
2. Creation of revenue neutral rate (RNR).
3. Centre will levy IGST on inter-State supply of goods and services. Import of goods will be subject to basic customs duty and IGST.
4. GST would be defined as any tax on supply of goods and services other than on alcohol for human consumption.
5. Central taxes like Central excise duty, additional excise duty, service tax, additional custom duty and special additional duty and State level taxes like VAT or sales tax, Central sales tax, entertainment tax, entry tax, purchase tax, luxury tax and octroi will subsume in GST.
6. Petroleum and petroleum products, i.e. crude, high speed diesel, motor spirit, aviation turbine fuel and natural gas shall be subject to the GST on a date to be notified by the GST Council.
7. 1 percent origin-based additional tax to be levied on inter-State supply of goods will be non-creditable in the GST chain. The revenue from this tax is to be assigned to the origin State. This tax is proposed to be levied for initial two years or such period as recommended by the GST Council.
8. Provision for removing imposition of entry tax/octroi across India.
9. Entertainment tax, imposed by States on movie theatres etc. will be subsumed in GST, but taxes on entertainment at panchayat, municipality or district level to continue.
10. GST may be levied on the sale of newspapers and advertisements and this would give the government, access

to substantial incremental revenues.

11. Stamp duties, typically imposed on legal agreements by the States, will continue to be levied by the States.
12. Administration of GST will be the responsibility of the GST Council, which will be the apex policy making body for GST. Members of GST Council comprise of the Central and State ministers in charge of the finance portfolio (EY, 2015).

While studying the provisions, one cannot overlook the positive aspects in the GST Bill:

1. It provides tax burden to split equitably between the manufacturing and the services.
2. It will work on the principle of point of sale/consumption thereby reducing the cascading effects or the double taxation system.
3. May be, it presents a picture of corruption free and transparent system.
4. It will decrease the goods prices and thereby increase the demands for goods, thus generating the employment and market for goods.

Besides the above justification, Yogita Beri (2011) provides base by commenting on the CENVAT which does not include additional customs duty, surcharges etc., thus keeping the benefits of comprehensive input tax and service tax set-off out of reach for manufacturers. The introduction of GST will not only include comprehensively more indirect taxes and integrate goods and services taxes but will also lead to revenue gain by widening the dealer base by capturing value addition in the distributive trade and increased compliance (Beri, 2011). She held that at present, there are some taxes like entertainment tax and luxury tax which are not subsumed in the state-VAT scheme. In fact, in the GST, the cascading effect is removed from CENVAT and services tax by establishing the set-off from original producer's point and service provider's point till the retailer's level. That is why, to give authority to States to tax on services, a Constitutional

Amendment Bill (115 and 122) is required. Analyzing the SGST, it will give extra power to States to levy on services plus removing the burden of Central sales tax (CST) (Beri, 2011).

The Constitutional Amendment Bill too gave a compensatory support to States for in case of loss of revenue to be appropriated by the Centre for up to 5 years on appearing basis i.e. 100 percent for first 3 years, 75 percent for 4th year and 50 percent for the final year. The GST Council had been proposed by Article 279a which will be a joint forum of States and Centre functioning under the chairmanship of the Union Finance Minister with 2/3rd representatives from States and 1/3rd from the Centre and the decision to be taken by a 2/3rd majority (Jain, 2015).

Critically evaluating the GST policy, one can say that IMF type of reforms, i.e. *one-size-fits-all* cannot be practiced in India given the different economic and political conditions of the regions. Accepting the different aspirations and the needs of States' desire, some customization of GST on the part of the Centre to conglomerate and erect an integrated taxation policy is required. India is certainly having diverse and differential capacity in terms of manufacturing and agricultural set up; like if we compare Mumbai with Punjab and Haryana or Bengaluru with Bihar and U.P., the economic and resource set up of these States compels statesmen to rethink before finally coming up with any new policy. In the light of above statements, we are analyzing the implications of GST under two sections i.e., political and economic respectively.

Political Implication

The task of integration of the taxes on goods and services in a federal structure is not an easy cakewalk. The Constitution of India, 1950, provides demarcation of taxing powers of the Centre and the States with manufacturing and import in the Centre's hand leaving post-manufacturing levies to the States. None of the States want to subdue their fiscal autonomy or the determining authority with regards to taxation as net exporter States does not want to subdue their tax threshold limit for the net consumer States.

Thus, the very concept of fiscal federalism is open to all and at the hands of net exporter States to set the rules of the game. More importantly, GST is acting as an invader for the fiscal federalism (GST India, 2015). The contentious issue is arriving at a consensus on the inter-State trade and commerce where services originating in one State and consumed in other State and the mechanism to share that revenues if it is possible, needs structural adjustment. The proposed GST structure (Article 279a, Section 12 of the 2014 Bill) too presents a dubious picture where adjudication is in the hands of GST Council by making it a dispute resolution body thereby countering the very Apex Court existence. If this will follow then the net producing States will try to overpower their interest at the cost of the net consumer States thereby working against the co-operative federalism (Beri, 2011).

In the words of Professor Kavita Rao (National Institute of Public finance and Policy), GST council will administer fixing of rates for CGST and SGST and so the individual States will lose their right to tax whichever commodities they want at their specific interest. Economist Prabhat Patnaik pointed out that States will be alienated from their limited autonomy of taxing like in the case of sales tax which accounted for 80 percent of their revenue (Sampant, 2015). Thus, the roadmap for GST to stand in compliance with fiscal federalism and co-operative federalism needs streamlining of the existing tax architecture instead of creating a new one.

Economic Implications

The bone of contention relates to inclusion of purchase taxes on food grains, taxes on motor spirit and high speed diesel (HSD), and octroi or entry tax. The food grain surplus States have been levying the purchase tax, the burden of which is exported to non-residents. The States are reluctant to bring motor spirit and high speed diesel within the ambit, as presently the tax is levied at a floor rate of 20 percent and the States derive about 35 percent of their sales tax collections from these petroleum products (Rao, 2014). Next in the line is the issue of revenue neutral rate (RNR). Revenue neutral rate are the rates that try to counter the deficit or no loss or gain of revenue. But how to reach an agreement is a complex work when the States are given the option of dual rate system i.e. one for necessary goods and items and other for general ones. Besides it, there also exists exemption list on which consensus among States needs to achieve. Similarly, the provision of compensation needs special attention as the Bill does not provide an answer to problem of compensation after 5 years if that persists.

Moreover, as per Professor Arun Kumar (CESP/JNU), this provision is in itself contradictory. He pointed out that India's revenue deficits hover around US$ 450 billion in comparison to US$ 350 billion foreign exchange reserve, so it is not possible for the state to meet the compensatory demands provisions. Instead, he suggests to tax the black market which is touching around 60 percent of the GDP, that can bring surplus revenue thus giving an alternative to GST (Kumar, 2013). Another major area of negotiation is tax on services with inter-State coverage where principle of origin rules, but clear cut rules for revenue appropriation and clearly defined principles can avoid future hindrance. Lastly, the issue of nationalization of single integrated market can phase out small businesses and local markets in international market competition.

Social Implication

The GST can work at best with minimal or zero exemption i.e. keeping the essential commodities out of the exemption list like in the case of New Zealand. Keeping GST rate low by increasing the number of goods and services under its purview could lead to taxing some essential goods at a higher rate which will hit lower income groups harder. So, neither a welfare state like India can think of cutting of welfare schemes nor will an elected government be ready to bear its consequences.

The Thirteenth Finance Commission 2010, opined for a 12 percent GST (7 percent SGST and 5 percent CGST) while the 2014 Bill pegs it at 27 percent. Both are unrealistic, as at 12 percent GST, some States will have to incur losses because some States' VAT touches around 13-14 percent and while at 27 percent it will be a burden for wage earners (Sampant, 2015).

Conclusion

Given the differential positioning of the states in India and the GST structure, it is a Herculean task to bring 32 players at par (29 states, 2 UTs and the Centre) but even if all the players reach to a consensus then that tax rate would be far from realistic (Govind, R., 2014). In fact, such a structure of GST cannot be found anywhere where both the Centre and the States has the authority to levy (Bird, 2010). It is legitimate for the state to negotiate for the fiscal autonomy but at the same time should not delve in predatory competition and export the burden of tax on the non-residents.

The issue of GST should not be dealt as between political parties rather be viewed as between Centre and the States if a pragmatic understanding is required. Pragmatically, India is marred by the previous taxation policy and as a result giving space to black market. However, at the same time, a policy restructuring is a call of the time to change the contours of the state.

Endnotes

1. Sun Belt refers to the states which act as manufacturing unit.
2. Rust belt refers to the states which act as consumer.

References

Beri, Y. (2011), "Problems and Prospects of Goods and Services Tax in India", *Economic Affairs*, pp. 353-357.

Bird, R. (2010), "VAT in Developing and Transitional Countries", New York: Cambridge University Press.

Govind, M.R. (2011), "Goods and Services Tax: A Gorilla, Chimpanzee or a Genus like Primates?", *Economic and Political Weekly*, pp. 43-48.

Govind, R. (2014), "Goods and Services Tax in India: Challenges and Prospects", retrieved from Ideas for India.

Jain, S. (2015), "Goods and Services Tax (GST): Concepts and Impact", available at: gstindia.com: www.gstindia.com/goods-st-gst-concept-impact.

Kumar, A. (2013), "India's Economy since Independence: Persisting Colonial Disruptions", Delhi: Vision Books.

Phukan, R. (2015), "GST Bill in India: One Step toward Simplifying the Muddled up Tax System", retrieved from mapsofindia.com.

Rao, G. (2014), "Ideas for India", available at: www.ideasforindia.in/articleprint.aspx.

Sampant, G. (2015), "GST: Good for Business, Snag for Federalism", *The Hindu*.

15

GST: Concepts, Model and Status

Shashi Sawhney

GST stands for goods and services tax. GST is also known by the name of value added tax (VAT) in some countries. GST/VAT can be defined as a consumption-based tax wherein the basic principle is to tax the value addition at each and every business stage.

GST is levied on all transactions carried out in the name of goods and services. To achieve this, tax paid on purchases is allowed as a set-off/credit against liability on output/income. Thus, in principle, the terms 'goods' and 'services' are not to be differentiated.

France was the first country to introduce the concept of GST and now more than 160 countries have introduced and implemented it. Most of the countries, depending upon their socio-economic formation, have introduced national level GST or dual GST.

GST differs from the existing tax structure in several ways. Under the current tax regime, the terms goods and services are treated differently.

As per the current system, 'goods' attract excise at the manufacturing level and VAT is levied at the time of sale. Whereas, services attract only one type of levy i.e. service tax on value of taxable services. However, under GST, both goods and services would be treated at par for taxing purposes.

The author tries to compile and summarize all important pieces of legislation together.

This paper covers all the key areas about GST, steps to be taken for making 'GST ready', timing/occurrence of events, etc. in an articulate manner. This paper will help the reader to easily understand the distinctions of GST. Finally, conclusions have been drawn regarding the effect of GST on the Indian economy.

Introduction

Modifications/reforms are an ever evolving and a continuous process. This statement is very much true in case of indirect tax regime where there is a close link with public and the general economy.

The system of key reforms and liberalization started way back in 1986 when MODVAT was introduced and is being continued since then. The concept of GST/VAT as a tax system has been accepted and preferred in most of the countries.

India is also making a move towards introduction of GST by taking steps/initiatives such as introduction of State VAT in India (from 2003 to 2008), integration of Central level CENVAT (in 2004) and introduction of negative list in service tax (in 2012).

GST has been in news over the last few years. Now, most of the key aspects of the proposed GST regime are already in public domain through various documents such as the 122nd Constitutional Amendment Bill, 2014, Reports on registration, payment, refunds and returns etc. Thus, it has become imperative for everyone to understand GST as it is expected to become a reality in the coming future.

GST would prove to be a game changing reform for the Indian economy by developing a common Indian market and reducing the cascading effect of tax on the cost of goods and services.

It will have a direct impact on the tax structure, tax incidence, tax computation, tax payment, compliance, credit utilization and reporting, thereby leading to a complete overhaul of the current indirect tax system.

Noteworthy Features of GST

GST Applicable on Supply: In GST regime, any "supply" in the form of sale, transfer, barter, lease, import of services etc. of goods and/or services made for a consideration will attract CGST (to be levied by Centre) and SGST (to be levied by the State).

As GST will be levied on 'supply' stated above, erstwhile taxable events such as 'manufacture', 'sale', 'provision of services' etc. will lose their relevance.

Further, if any 'supply' is done without a consideration, such as permanent transfer of business assets, self-supply of goods or services, assets retained after deregistration etc. then it will attract GST.

Amusingly, even a 'barter' system transaction which was previously untaxed in VAT regime, will now be covered under the GST.

GST Payable as per Time of Supply: The liability to pay CGST/SGST will arise at the time of 'supply' as determined for goods and services.

In this regard, separate provisions have been made defining the time of supply for goods and services. The provisions contemplate payment of GST at the earliest for: (a) Goods: dispatch of goods, receipt of payment, issuance of invoice or date on which buyer shows receipt of goods, (b) Services: issuance of invoice, receipt of payment or date on which service recipient presents receipt of services.

Thus, it can be said that determining the 'time' of supply for taxation purposes and further maintaining reconciliation between revenue as per financials and as per GST rules could be a major challenge to cope up with.

Determining the Place of Supply: At present, inter-State supply of goods attract Central sales tax. Now, it provides that an inter-State supply of goods and/or services will be covered under IGST (i.e. CGST plus SGST). Thus, an 'intra-State' or 'inter-State' transaction needs to be determined as taxes will be levied accordingly.

In this regard, the draft GST law provides separate provisions which will help an assessee in determining the place of supply for goods and services. For 'goods', the place of supply would be location of delivery of goods. Whereas for 'services' the place of supply would be location of service recipient.

However, there are multiple scenarios such as supply of services in relation to immovable property etc. wherein this generic principle will not be applicable and specific rule will determine the pace of supply.

Thus, the business will have to scroll through all the provisions governing place of supply before determining the same.

Valuation under GST: Calculation of GST would be based on the 'transaction value'. Transaction value can be defined as the price actually paid or payable for the said supply of goods and/or services between unrelated parties.

The transaction value is said to include all other expenses incurred with respect to sales such as packing, commission etc. Even subsidies linked to supply will be includable while determining the transaction value. Discounts/incentives, if any, will form part of 'transaction value' if they are allowed after supply is affected.

However, discounts/incentives given before or at the time of supply will be permissible as deduction from transaction value.

The valuation rules appear to be drafted by taking few provisions from current valuation provisions in excise (for e.g. concept of 'transaction value'), service tax (for e.g. concept of 'pure agent') and customs (for e.g. concept of 'goods of like kind and quality').

Input Tax Credit under GST: Under the current CENVAT credit regime, CENVAT credit on various services such as motor vehicle related services, catering services, employee insurance, construction of civil structure etc. is disallowed.

This denial of credits leads to unnecessary cost burden on the assessee. It was expected that in GST regime, seamless credit will be allowed to business houses without any denial or any restrictions except say goods/services which are availed for personal use other than official use (somewhat similar to Unite Kingdom VAT laws).

However, the aforesaid credit would continue to be unavailable under GST as well (in respect of both goods and services).

Further, credit is proposed to be disallowed on goods and/or services used for private or personal consumption, to the extent they are so consumed.

This continuation of denial will lead to substantial tax cascading (as rate of GST will be higher that the current rate of service tax).

Introduction of 33 New GST Laws: In GST regime, there will be one CGST law, 31 SGST laws for each of the States including two Union Territories and one IGST law governing inter-State supplies of goods and services.

Rate of GST Not Yet Specified in the Draft GST Law: The rate of GST in draft GST law has not been specified till date. However, various news reports suggest that the revenue neutral rate (RNR) as proposed by the Chief Economic Advisor Shri Arvind Subramanian could be 17-18 percent. Further, there could be a lower rate (of 12-14 percent) for concessional goods and a higher rate (up to 40 percent) for luxury goods (such as luxury cars, tobacco products etc.).

Time Limit for Show Cause Notices (SCN): Time limit for issuance of SCN in generic cases (i.e. other than fraud, suppression etc.) would be 3 years and in cases of fraud, suppression etc. it would be 5 years.

It is important to note that the time limit prescribed for issuance of SCN for generic cases is much more than the current time limit prescribed in excise law (i.e. 12 months) and service tax legislation (i.e. 18 months).

This will give much scope to the authorities while issuing

SCN and a bunch of problems to assessees for three years.

Old Provisions Re-introduced: Most of the current provisions such as reverse charge, tax deduction, pre-deposit, prosecution, arrest etc. have been continued in the proposed draft GST law.

The new GST law seems to be a new wine in the same old bottle as most of the current inefficiencies have been continued within the proposed GST law.

Possible Impact on the Businesses and Consumers

The introduction of GST would lead to an exemplary shift in indirect tax regime and would require business enterprises to take a close look at their current and future business models.

Quantifying and evaluating its impact on the vertical and/or horizontal integration of business enterprises is need of the hour.

In a nutshell, the following conclusions can be drawn from the above discussion.

Change in Tax Base and the Taxable Value: Since, both CGST and SGST shall be levied on same tax base, therefore both would be charged on the same taxable value.

This is altogether different from the current scheme of taxation where Central taxes like excise and Central sales tax are first charged on the basic value of goods and then State taxes are charged on a value which is inclusive of basic value and Central taxes already charged at the Central level by the authorities.

Once GST is introduced, both CGST and SGST will be charged on same taxable amount leading to substantial reduction in payment of total tax amount.

Substantial Influence on Prices of Goods and Services in Business 2 Business (B2B) Segment: The basic principles of GST would be similar to VAT principles.

Hence, any amount paid as input tax would be allowed as credit against the amount payable as output tax. GST thereby would have a significant effect on profitability of businesses.

Incidence on Prices of Goods and Services in Business 2 Customer (B2C) Segment: Although under GST, tax base will widen and dual taxes in the form of CGST and SGST will be applicable, but since tax credits will be available to all the participants in B2B segment, it is anticipated that final prices of the industrial goods for the consumers may get reduced.

However, it is anticipated that the overall prices of the services offered in B2C segment may increase. This is because the combined rate of CGST and SGST is higher than the rate of service tax being charged at present.

Availability of Benefit of Input Tax Credit in the Entire Value Chain: The amount of tax paid as input tax would be allowed as credit against the payment of output tax throughout the logistics chain for supply of goods which will provide significant additional credits which are currently missed out on purchases from traders, who are not registered under excise.

Further, the amount of service tax paid on SGST will now be available for set-off against SGST on goods. This would prove to be a big relief for the traders who pay VAT or excise as output tax and do not get any credit for service tax paid by them on input services.

Impact on Strategic Business Decisions: With the imposition of GST, production process of any business enterprise can easily be broken at every stage of production into different segments and there would not be any impact on the total taxes paid by that company.

One can decide to outsource its production process or entire production activity only by considering the feasibility and profitability as per other factors. Make or buy decisions would not be impacted because tax structure would be uniform and simplified.

Benefit of Economies of Scale and Division of Labour: Just to comply with the tax laws, business units will not be forced to do anything in which they are inefficient/face difficulties in performing the same.

They can concentrate on the things in which they are best

fitted and can increase their efficiencies by working upon it.

Unutilized and Accumulated Credits of Service Tax, Input Excise and VAT at the Effective Date of Introduction of GST: The Government is in talks that while transforming the tax structure, the provisions in relation to the carry forward and set-off of accumulated CENVAT credit and VAT credit which will remain unutilized on GST effective date, will be in place. Thus, loss of this accumulated credit is not likely to happen/take place.

Different Levels of Threshold: This is explained with an example below:

Taxable turnover of a small manufacturer 'A'—below ₹ 10 lakh.

Taxable turnover of medium dealer 'B'—below ₹ 50 lakh.

Taxable turnover of a large dealer 'C'—above ₹ 150 lakh.

Now, if A sells goods to consumers directly, his goods will not be afflicted by any GST, but if he sells to B, the same goods will afflict SGST and if he sells to C, the same goods will afflict CGST as well as SGST.

Thus, same goods manufactured by A will attract different tax treatments.

Transfers to Branches and Job Work Transactions and Their Treatment: The draft discussion paper on GST is concerned with the imposition of GST on all transactions of Goods and Services made for consideration. But, in the case of transfer of goods to branch offices and at place of job work, the paper is silent.

However, there could be two options for the treatment of this. One option could be the imposition of IGST on such transactions. The second option could be to transfer the stock at zero rate instead of exempting the same.

Registration

- There will be state-specific single registration for Central GST (CGST), Integrated GST (IGST) and State GST (SGST). Multiple registrations in a State for business verticals would also be permitted.

- Registration number would be a PAN-based 15-digit alpha-numeric registration number.
- Registration would be granted through common GST portal.
- Registration would be deemed to be approved if not rejected.

Payments

- Taxpayer will be required to make payment of CGST, SGST, IGST and additional tax through internet banking.
- Over-the-counter payment could be permissible only for payments up to ₹ 10,000 per challan.
- For making e-payment, GST taxpayer will be required to access goods and services tax network (GSTN) for generation of the challan where basic details of the tax payer will be auto populated.

Refunds

- Under certain situations, such as exports, excess payment by mistake, refund of pre-deposit, and refund to international tourists, the taxpayer can claim refund of GST paid.
- For export of goods, an exporter should procure goods on payment of appropriate GST, and then claim refund from the respective governments.
- Duty-free inputs for exported goods may not be available.

References

Asia Pulse News (2007), "Framework for Indian GST Regime Likely Ready by September", July 18.

Concept Note on GST, Ministry of Finance, available at: http://dor.gov.in/Gstintro, accessed on March 16, 2016.

Economic Times (2015), "India Inc Backs Finance Minister Arun Jaitley's Call for Quick Execution of Tax Reforms", December 18.

Indian Express (2009), "A Good and Simple Tax", August 5.

Pritam Mahure (2015), "What is the Draft GST Law all About", *The*

Hindu Business Line, December 11.

Part V:
GST: Political Challenges

16

GST: The Challenges Ahead

Vichitra Gupta

Introduction

Goods and services tax being the largest indirect tax reform since 1947 is aimed at promoting economic integration of India. It shall facilitate uniform tax levied on goods and services across the country. Presently, the indirect tax system in India is complicated with overlapping taxes imposed separately by the Centre and the States. According to Finance Minister, Mr. Arun Jaitley, the GST will be instrumental in helping the GDP of India to grow by about 2 percent. It shall offer solution to the multinationals as it breaks down the indirect tax structure into one single tax payable by the companies.

The main contentious issue in the GST Bill is the feared loss of fiscal power to States. The Bill has also proposed a GST Council wherein all he Union and State ministers in-charge of finance shall be placed on equal footing. It shall also have a Dispute Settlement Authority to resolve the tensions between the Centre and the States. Cooperation from the State governments would possibly be one of the key factors for successful implementation of the GST Bill. Main opposition party, Congress, wants 18 percent of GST cap to be included in the Bill while the FM and most of the States do not agree with this as in case of any change required in the figure in future, the whole amendment procedure needs to be followed again.

GST, once implemented, shall be a transparent and efficient system that would blur the demarcation between goods and services and shall boost the private sector.

GST: Objectives and Features

Goods and Services Bill is aimed at transforming India into a uniform market. It would break down the indirect tax structure and current fiscal barrier between the States. Under the present indirect tax system, there is the overlapping of taxes levied by the Centre and the States. By intertwining all the taxes into one, the goods and services tax is the greatest tax reform since 1947. GST is to be levied on the consumption and not on the production of goods. According to Shri Arun Jaitley, the Finance Minister of India, "The GST bill will lead to the economic integration of India. By levying a uniform tax on goods and services, it shall facilitate smooth and uninterrupted movement of goods all over the country".

The GST shall be levied on the intra-State and inter-State supply and consumption of goods and the import of goods and services. GST shall be a boon for multinational companies also. It shall promote present government's motto of 'ease of doing business' as it shall break down the indirect tax structure being levied at different levels and integrate all the taxes into one single tax payable by the companies. Export oriented businesses shall also get a boost as GST shall not be levied on goods and services exported from India. The GST while eliminating multiple taxes on a product from the stage of production in one State to the consumption in other States, shall also reduce the final cost of the product. Once the cost of the product is down, consumption shall increase. With more consumers on the scene, the production shall be boosted on one hand and on the other hand government shall also be able to generate more revenue as the number of taxpayers will increase.

GST is to be collected on the value added goods at each stage of sale and purchase in the supply chain. But at each next stage, the manufacturer, wholesaler and retailer shall recover. Increased buoyancy shall improve tax collection. The cost of tax collection shall also be less as the tax collecting departments are going to be reduced under GST. Most of the tax collection work will be online. Tax rate under GST shall be less but the number of assesses would increase as more business entities would come under the tax purview. Companies that are in unorganized sector shall come under the tax regime. Hence, the tax base is going to be widened which would further lead to increase in better revenue collection. According to the Finance Minister, "The GST shall be instrumental in helping the GDP of India to grow by 2 percent".

GST is to be collected on the value added goods at each stage of sale and purchase in the supply chain. But at each next stage the manufacturer, wholesaler and retailer shall recover the GST in the form of tax credits. Consumer, the last person in the chain shall bear the tax. Since all the persons in the supply chain are claiming back the amount paid in tax through tax credit mechanism, that amount shall not be added to the price of the product. Hence, it will reduce the final cost for the consumer. At present, the tax system has a very complicated regime where certain overlapping taxes are levied by the Centre and States, both separately. The GST, if implemented, shall transform India into a single uniform market. Certain products such as alcohol, tobacco, petroleum products may be put out of the GST regime.

The GST shall have three kinds of taxes, Central, State and the integrated GST for intra-State transactions. Both Centre and States shall be equally empowered to collect their respective taxes. Thus, both are empowered equally under CGST and SGST. Taxes such as VAT, Central sales tax, excise duty, entry tax, octroi, service tax etc. shall be absorbed in a single tax. Octroi, at present levied in six states (Gujarat, Himachal Pradesh, Maharashtra, Punjab and Rajasthan), varies from 5-6 percent of the product value.

State Government levies octroi as and when the product enters the State and the charges fluctuate in each State as per the government regulations. The product's cost gets increased due to different rates of tax in different States. GST shall do away with all such problems. The overlapping of Central and state taxes raises the tax burden of the products that makes them less competitive in the international markets. Due to the multiple tax rates, laws and processes, common man sometimes fails to comply with such complex legislation and adopts tax evasive practices. Hence, loss of revenue is inevitable. The cascading effect of taxes i.e. the taxation over taxes amounts to slump in the supply chain of manufacturers→ wholesalers→retailer→consumer, ultimately leading to inflation.

Under GST, no distinction is made between goods and services. There shall be lower tax rate, transparent and corruption-free tax system where exemptions are going to be minimized. GST shall be levied at the destination point. At present, a manufacturer pays tax when the product moves out of his factory and again it is taxed at the retail outlet. Under GST, the tax paid by the manufacturer and retailer shall be claimed back as tax credits. The combined GST rate is expected to be around 14-16 percent.

Currently, the indirect tax on most of the products including service tax comes to around 20 percent. The benefits of reduced tax shall be passed on to the consumers. Consequently, the prices shall expectedly fall. The estimated gain India will get may be US$ 15 billion a year with the implementation of GST Bill as it is going to promote exports, encourage multinationals, raise employment level and boost overall growth. By raising employment, purchasing power of individuals shall increase and by lowering of prices due to less tax burden, more consumption shall be there leading to more production and the circle of growth moving thereby.

History of GST

The Vajpayee Government, in 2000, set up the Empowered Committee of State Finance Ministers to decide major changes in the taxation system. The Committee headed by Asim Dasgupta, West Bengal Minister for Finance facilitated a switch over from Central excise duty and State level sales tax model to a VAT model. The Committee also designed the blueprint of GST. The Kelkar Task Force set up for implementation of Fiscal Responsibility and Budget Management Act, 2003, realized that the existing system of taxation of goods and services needs to be reformed. The task force suggested a comprehensive goods and services tax that would blur the demarcation between goods and services.

In the Budget speech of the financial year 2006-07, a proposal was given to introduce a national level Goods and Services Tax by April 1, 2010. The responsibility of formulating the design of GST was assigned to the Empowered Committee of State Finance Ministers. In April 2008, EC submitted a report containing recommendation about structure and design of GST. The report was titled as "A Model and Roadmap for Goods and Services Tax in India". In November 2009, EC released its first discussion paper on GST so as to invite a debate on the topic and to gain inputs from the stakeholders.

Again to take the GST-related work further, a joint working group was formed that consisted of officers from Central as well as State governments. This was further divided into three sub-committees: (i) to work on draft legislations, (ii) processes to be decided in the implementation of GST, and (iii) the Empowered Group for developing IT systems under Nandan Nilekani. In 2009, the UPA government opened a discussion on GST Bill by introducing it in the Parliament but the Bill could not be passed. The NDA government reintroduced the Bill in December 2014 with slight changes in the draft. After much deliberation the Bill was passed on August 8, 2016 in Lok Sabha and on August 3, 2016 in the Rajya Sabha.

As the GST bill affects the federal structure that amounts to the basic structure of the Constitution and thereby needs to be passed by two-thirds majority in both the Houses and to be ratified by half of the State assemblies.

Contentious Issues in the Bill

The main troublesome issue now is the fear of the States of losing their fiscal powers and financial autonomy. Since GST is a consumption-based tax, the States having higher consumption shall gain better revenues whereas the States that are manufacturing the product shall lose. The backward and less-developed States that do not have too much purchasing power of people shall face a major fall in revenue collection. The States that have more labour and natural resources to produce something but not able to consume due to lack of purchasing power shall never be developed due to loss of revenue. Some States also fear that if uniform tax rate gets lower than the existing tax rate, their revenue collection shall be down. Many state governments such as that of Madhya Pradesh, Chhattisgarh and Tamil Nadu have reservations against the Bill.

For a smooth transition to GST, cooperation from States is urgently required. To do away the fears of States, the Bill has proposed 100 percent compensation packages for three years for any revenue loss, 75 percent in the fourth year and 50 percent in the fifth year. But the States were not satisfied with this package and in June 2015 they put up a demand of 100 percent compensation for all five years. The Cabinet Committee on Economic Affairs cleared an amendment by which the states could get full compensation for five years. This move shall bring most of the States around GST. Levying 1 percent additional tax on the supply of goods is a major sticky point where some States do not agree.

Though this provision is beneficial for the States which have a strong manufacturing base, it is opposed by States who say that this system would go against the spirit of the GST system—of the consolidated tax if we keep on adding the piecemeal levies on it. Chief Economic advisor Arvind Subramaniam had also warned of the negative impact of such additional tax. The provision of 1 percent additional tax has been added to the Bill to compensate for the investment the

States had already done in the manufacturing sector. Regarding this, the cabinet has taken decision to exempt the stock transfers within group companies from this additional tax, but overall, the additional tax shall remain. The additional 1 percent tax shall go to the States for two years in the course of inter-State trade.

Another contentious issue in the implementation of GST is the revenue kitty of municipal bodies and nagar panchayats. Under the present format of the Bill, the civic bodies shall receive the revenue out of state revenue only. Shiv Sena, though an ally of BJP, opposes it on the grounds that BMC (Brihan Mumbai Municipal Corporation) that is receiving ₹ 8,000 crore annually through octroi shall be cash starved under the GST regime and as such may not be able to take up development projects. BMC spends the major amount of octroi revenue on a number of development projects at present. Hence, Shiv Sena asserts that the government should ensure that there is no major revenue loss. Moreover, funds should be made available to them directly and not through the State. The Cabinet has been handling the contentious issues judiciously and at a fast speed as GST is one of the most significant of the tax reforms.

Passage of the GST Bill and the Roadblocks Faced

The Lok Sabha passed the 122nd Constitutional Amendment—Goods and Services Tax Bill on May 6, 2015. Rajya Sabha passed the same Bill with 9 amendments on August 3, 2016 and the Lok Sabha again passed the modified Bill on August 8, 2016, approving all the 9 amendments by the Rajya Sabha. Since the Bill is going to affect the federal autonomy, it has to go through major Constitutional Amendment clause i.e. the passage of bill by two-thirds majority in both the Houses and then ratification by half of the State assemblies.

The main opposition party, Congress had put up a demand for certain modifications such as the GST rate to be capped at

18 percent and the same to be included in Amendment Bill. The government, on the other hand, is of the opinion that the tax rate cannot be written in the Bill as it would be difficult to change the tax rate if required in future. For that, again the whole amendment procedure shall be required. The task of deciding of rate from time to time shall be left to the GST Council that is being represented by the Centre and States both. Congress further wants that the proposed 1 percent levy on inter-State trade be removed and an independent dispute resolution mechanism are evolved for the States.

Earlier, Finance Minister Arun Jaitley in an interview to All India Radio asserted that he is trying his level best to convince the Congress leaders to bring them around GST, but even if Congress party continues to oppose it, the Bill shall be put to vote. [2] But to put the amendment bill to vote, the House is required to be in order. Congress party possessing the numeric strength had the power to disrupt the House and any disruption would have stalled the passage of the Bill. Hence, the government continued to struggle to get GST Bill passed.

With 53 Rajya Sabha members just retired and after June 11 2016 elections, Congress was the biggest loser and BJP had gained certain seats though it still fell short of the majority mark. The composition of House had changed only marginally in favour of BJP. NDA then banked upon the regional players to get GST Bill passed. NDA would benefit a lot from the presence of regional parties getting dominant position in the June biennial elections. Trinamool Congress Chief Mamta Banerjee, after being convinced by the PM came forward in support of the GST.

Left parties were also indicative of the support to GST during the meetings between FM and the Kerala CM. Pinnarayi Vijayan, Bihar Chief Minister Nitish Kumar and Odisha's Navin Patnaik have been supporters of GST due to the anticipated gains the respective states are going to get due to GST. Odisha's BJD though has deep concerns over royalties for minerals but supports the Bill with its 7 members. Lalu Prasad Yadav's RJD gaining more seats in Rajya Sabha would also push for the GST as they are its supporters. But on the other hand, BJP allies such as Shiv Sena (3 seats), Telugu Desam Party (6 seats) and Akali Dal (3 seats) were relatively smaller in Rajya Sabha as against its rivals such as Janta Dal (U) that had 13 and Trinamool Congress with a strength of 12 seats.

Due to recently developed cordial relations with AIADMK, NDA was hopeful of getting its support but Tamil Nadu has certain concerns over the Bill. The State with a strong manufacturing base is strongly worried about the loss of revenue. Though the Finance Minister has tried to convince Jayalalitha that the compensation clause would certainly resolve the issue, Jayalalitha has urged that the Centre should strive for a broad consensus on important issues regarding GST. Finance Minister in his meeting with states representatives on June 14, 2016 addressed genuine apprehension of the States.

Tamil Nadu CM wanted a consensus on compensation period and methodology, revenue neutral rates, commodities to be excluded from GST and IGST, model and clarity on dual administrative control so that the genuine apprehensions of the States regarding loss of fiscal autonomy and permanent revenue loss are alleged. [2] Moreover, Tamil Nadu strongly objects to the provision of GST Council as it would jeopardise the autonomy of States in fiscal matters. She favours the combination of existing mechanism of Empowered Committee of State Ministers that deals with VAT. The voting pattern and decision-making in GST Council is not at all acceptable to them. That gives the Central government an effective veto in GST Council as no distinction is sought to be made among the States in weightage. If at all the Council is formed, the weightage of the vote of Central government should be reduced to one-fourth of the total votes cast and that of the States correspondingly increased to three-fourths. Further, the weightage of each State's vote should be in proportion to the representation of the State in Rajya Sabha. [3]

Moreover, in lieu of the proposed 1 percent tax on inter-

State supply of goods, the origin States must be allowed to retain 4 percent of the Central GST part of the inter-State GST that would be leviable on inter-State supply of goods and services as this would ensure speedy recompensation for a portion of the revenue loss and will reduce the amount of compensation payable. [4] The most important demand of Tamil Nadu being the constitutionally mandated independent compensation mechanism for full 100 percent compensation for revenue losses suffered by the States for a period of five years is already considered by the FM. States are also trying to seek bargains in return for providing support to GST Bill such as Tamil Nadu seeking centre's support in lifting the stay on bull taming sport, Jallikattu, constitution of Cauvery Management Board etc.

Punjab Finance Minister Parminder Singh Dhindsa agreed to GST while saying that the issues like compensatory mechanism for GST and dual control may be debated later but we have agreed to go ahead with the GST. [5] Sh. Arun Jaitley said in the June 14 meeting that every participant had agreed to the basic idea of GST implementation. Jaitley assured States that any notional loss suffered by the States on account of a switch to the GST regime will be compensated by the Centre. He also announced the flexibility of the government on the demand for scrapping a 1 percent additional tax on inter-State sale, adding that it will lead to higher outgo from the Centre to the producing States. West Bengal Finance Minister Amit Mishra, head of the Empowered Committee announced that the panel shall again meet in the month of July to discuss the two contentious issues where consensus is elusive: (i) revenue neutral rate calculation (a tax rate at which States do not lose revenue), and (ii) the issue of dual control (businesses having to file details of sale transactions with both the Central and state agencies).

The great achievement of June 14, 2016 meeting of FM with state representatives was the creation of a unanimous view among the States against specifying the cap of 18 percent in Constitutional amendment bill. States were of the view that the cap should not be specified in the amendment bill because the contingencies might arise in future. Once it is fixed, it will be difficult to change it in future without a further amendment. Cap of 18 percent of GST rate to be specified in the Bill is one of the three main demands of the opposition Congress.

Jaitley has asked Congress to allow the Parliamentary process to unfold in case it does not support the legislation and while this might be a part of psychological warfare, it also refers to the voting process. [6] So far, Congress has remained unmoved and the relations between the parties have remained tense with the Agusta Corruption case being the latest feud. Congress also says that the BJP did not allow the GST bill to go through when it was in opposition with states where it is in office like Gujarat and Madhya Pradesh opposing its provision. [7]

In order to make India an attractive investment destination, Jaitley said, "The government has undertaken several reforms and the pipeline remains robust with measures. The IT backbone required for implementing GST has made significant headway. The system will provide a standard interface for taxpayers including registration, filing of returns and payment of tax and a shared infrastructure between the Centre, the States and other bodies like RBI". [8]

Conclusion

GST once implemented shall be a transparent and efficient system that would blur the demarcation between goods and services. The integrated system of tax shall boost the private sector, promote multinationals and shall invite more FDI into the country, lower the prices of the products and increasing more and more consumability by increasing purchasing power through more employability and less tax. Though the tax shall be less, there shall be no loss of the revenue as more and more companies in unorganised sector shall come under the tax net. Due to increased IT base required for GST implementation, the educated youth shall gain more employment, leading India to an overall growth of GDP and control of inflation. GST on the whole shall help promoting the phase of neo-liberalism where more economic liberty shall boost the private sector and ultimately the economy of the nation.

Endnotes

1. PTI, May 16, 2016.
2. Manoj, C.G., Indian Express, June 14, 2016.
3. Manoj, C.G., op.cit.
4. Ibid.
5. Indian Express, June 15, 2016, p. 2.
6. Ibid.
7. Deshpande, Rajeev and Gupta, Surojit, "GST Bill Inches towards 213 Backing in Rajya Sabha", Times of India, June 8, 2016.
8. Deepshikha Sikarwar, Economic times Bureau, June 3, 2016.

References

"All You Need to Know about Goods and Services Tax", available at: http://www.thehindu.com/business/Industry/all-you-need-to-know-about-goods-and-services-tax/article7929788.ece.

"Freezing of GST Rate: Congress Shows First Signs of a Thaw", available at: http://indianexpress.com/article/india/india-news-india/freezing-of-gst-bill-rate-congress-shows-first-signs-of-a-thaw-2902432.

http://www.business-standard.com/article/economy-policy/what-is-gst-and-how-it-will-change-taxation-in-india-115050600828_1.html.

http://indianexpress.com/article/india/india-news-india/will-go-for-voting-on-gst-bill-if-congress-doesnt-come-onboard-arun-jaitley-2800936.

http://www.ndtv.com/india-news/more-collateral-damage-for-gst-bill-will-miss-another-deadline-1401649.

http://www.finmin.nic.in/reports/ModelGSTLaw_draft.pdf.

http://www.livemint.com/Politics/pBrzoISUIdEkTkxhEzfRtL/Govt-to-initiate-talks-with-Congress-on-GST-says-Arun-Jaitl.html.

http://articles.economictimes.indiatimes.com/2016-06-

14/news/73768070_1_gst-rate-indirect-tax-regime-state-finance-ministers.

Legislative Brief, "GST: The Constitutional Bill (2014)", PRS Legislative Research, available at: http://www.prsindia.org/billtrack/the-constitution-122nd-amendment-gst-bill-2014-3505.

"Monsoon Session of Parliament Might Pass GST Bill. What Does It Mean to You and Me?", available at: http://indiatoday.intoday.in/story/what-is-the-gst-what-are-salient-features-of-the-proposed-bill/1/533502.html.

"Monsoon Parliament Session to Commence from Today; GST Bill, Next RBI Head on Priority", available at: http://www.newsx.com/national/34776-prior-to-monsoon-parliament-session-congress-party-hints-at-dropping-key-gst-demand.

17

GST as a Game Changer

Suresh Kumar

Goods and services tax (GST) is the most talked about topic in the field of indirect taxation today in India. The GST in the developing countries has become a much debatable issue among the scholars. GST as a part of the market economy today connects to a market system aligned with information technology to produce a centralized system to integrate the taxation system in the country. The market demands the need for a single taxation system in India dealing with the Central government and all the respective State governments. It is a comprehensive tax levy on manufacture, sale and consumption of goods and services at the national level. This tax applies on goods and services with value addition at each stage having a comprehensive and continuous chain of set of benefits from the producer and the service provider, touching the retailer level with the customers bearing the tax.

GST is the product of a global mummy market and our government has taken the big reform initiative remoulding the present taxation system. Economically, India is a very rich country with abundant natural resources and a huge manpower. However, it is pertinent to note that a small group of population is paying taxes to the government and while a majority of the population is earning revenue from various sources but they are hiding their source of income. For example, a number of people in Delhi (such as students, business professionals, working class and part-time employees) are living in rented accommodation and surprisingly ninety percent of the landlords are not disclosing their income while filing their income tax return. The nonorganized sector such as retail marketing, local grocery shops etc. have a similar situation and come in the category of non-paying tax individuals. Therefore, black money market in India has been increasing day by day. Recently, Prime Minister Narendra Modi raised the same concern in his *Man ki Baat* radio programme and has given the opportunity to the black money holders to declare it by September 30, 2016.

Historically, GST was initiated by the UPA-II government but due to lack of mutual consensus among the political parties, it could not be passed at that time. However, under the present government, it was again initiated in the Parliament and was passed recently. The Lok Sabha passed the 122nd Constitutional Amendment—Goods and Services Tax Bill on May 6, 2015. Rajya Sabha passed the same Bill with 9 amendments on August 3, 2016 and the Lok Sabha passed the modified Bill on August 8, 2016, approving all the 9 amendments by the Rajya Sabha. Currently, the hope is that GST will be implemented from April 1, 2017.

It is anticipated that the GST tax base will be a comprehensive one and virtually all goods and services will be taxable with minimum exemptions.

GST will be a game changing reform for the Indian economy by developing a common Indian market and reducing the cascading effect of tax on the cost of goods and services. It will impact the tax structure, tax incidence, tax computation, tax payment, compliance, credit utilization and reporting, leading to a complete overhaul of the current indirect tax system.

GST will have a far reaching impact on almost all the aspects of the business operations in the country, for instance, pricing of products and services, supply chain optimization, IT, and accounting and tax compliance systems. As we know, GST has dual model of working like Central goods and services tax (CGST) which is the GST levied and collected by the Centre and State goods and services tax (SGST) which is GST levied and collected by the States/UTs while Integrated goods and services tax (IGST) that is GST for inter-State transactions, levied and collected by the Centre.

According to Ministry of Finance, the following is the roadmap for the GST in India:

- Reduce distortion in prices due to tax policies.
- Foster a common market across the country.
- Distribute the burden of taxation equitably between manufacturing and services.
- Lower the tax rate by broadening the tax base and reducing exemptions.
- Reduce the burden on the taxpayer by eliminating cascading of taxes at multiple levels.
- Simplify inter-State commerce.
- Encourage compliance, and discourage non-compliance.

India being a federal form of government, a three-tier system exists with a limited autonomy for taxation. Financially, State and local governments are dependent on the Centre but there are some areas where both governments can generate revenue independently. States in the country have two main reservations as regards the GST. The first is the loss of revenue. Many States want commodities such as petroleum and alcohol to be outside the purview of GST. Producing states fear that they will lose substantial revenue on account of GST being a destination based consumption tax. The second concern is the loss of autonomy like constitution of GST Council, dispute settlement authority, compensation mechanism and dual control.

The main argument is that GST is good for economic development but since Independence, three remarkable issues still remain challenging viz. poverty, unemployment and backwardness. Is it possible that through GST, the government can stop black marketing of goods and many such related practices? Is it possible that except government employees, earners from the various other sources will show their income while filing the ITR? And will GST lead to market reforms and generation of job opportunities?

However, GST if implemented would eliminate the cascading effects of taxes on production and distribution cost of goods and services. The exclusion of cascading effects on tax will significantly improve the competitiveness of goods and services in the market which will have a beneficial impact on the GDP of the country. It is felt that GST would serve a superior reason to achieve the objective of streamlining the indirect tax regime in India which can remove the cascading effects in supply chain till the level of final consumer.

18

Understanding Political Dimensions of GST

Prahlad Kumar Bairwa

Goods and services tax (GST) is a broad based and a single comprehensive tax levied on goods and services consumed in an economy. GST is levied at every stage of the production-distribution chain with applicable set-offs in respect of the tax remitted at previous stages. It is basically a tax on final consumption. GST is a value added tax to be implemented in India. GST is the only indirect tax that directly affects all sectors and sections of our economy. Since the introduction of this Bill, several State governments were criticizing this initiative of the Central government in the name of interference in state matters endangering the federal structure.

To facilitate the introduction of GST, the Lok Sabha passed the 122nd Constitutional Amendment—Goods and Services Tax Bill on May 6, 2015. Rajya Sabha passed the same Bill with 9 amendments on August 3, 2016. Lok Sabha passed the modified Bill on August 8, 2016, approving all the 9 amendments by the Rajya Sabha. The objective of the GST is to maintain a commonality between the basic structure and design of the CGST, SGST and SGST between States. In this article, we will focus on political understanding of this Bill and have tried to highlight the objectives, the proposed GST is trying to achieve. Thereafter, we have discussed the possible challenges and threats, and then, opportunities that GST brings before us to strengthen our free market economy.

Introduction

GST is a national level comprehensive tax levy on

manufacture, sale and consumption of goods and services. It is a tax on goods and services including value addition at each stage with comprehensive and continuous chain of set-off benefits from the producer's/service provider's point up to the retailer's level where only the final consumer should bear the tax. Necessity of introduction of a GST to replace the existing multiple tax structures of Central and State taxes is a desirable as well as imperative in the present emerging economic environment. Increasingly, services are used or consumed in production and distribution of goods and vice versa. Separate taxation of goods and services often requires splitting of transaction values into value of goods and services for taxation, which leads to greater complexities, administration and compliances costs. The positivity of the GST system is the integration of various taxes which makes it possible to give full credit for input taxes collected. GST will help in removing economic distortions and will help in development of a common national market.

Justifications of the GST

Followings are the justifications in favour of GST:

1. Credit for service tax paid is being allowed to manufacturer/service provider to a limited extent. In order to give the credit of service tax paid in respect of services consumed, it is necessary that there should be a comprehensive system under which both the goods and services are covered.
2. At present, the service tax is levied on restricted items only. It is to reduce the effect of cascading of taxes, which means levying tax on taxes.
3. Major defect is in the State VAT or the excise duty paid to the Central Government, which goes against the principle of not levying tax on taxes.
4. CENVAT is allowed on the value of goods to be taxed which is a cascading effect on account of CENVAT element.

5. Many of the States are still continuing with various types of indirect taxes, such as luxury tax, entertainment tax, etc.
6. As tax is being levied on inter-State transfer of goods, there is no provision for taking input credit on CST, leading to additional burden for the dealers.

The GST Model

1. Central GST.
2. State GST.

The dual GST model proposed by the Empowered Committee and accepted by the Centre will have dual system for imposing the tax.

Central excise duty, additional excise duty, services tax and additional duty of customs (equivalent to excise), state VAT, entertainment tax, taxes on lotteries, betting and gambling and entry tax (not levied by local bodies) would be subsumed within the GST.

Salient Features of GST

1. It would be applicable to all transactions of goods and services.
2. It is to be paid in the accounts of the Centre and the States separately.
3. The rules for taking and utilization of credit for the Central GST and the State GST would be aligned.
4. Cross utilization of ITC between the Central GST and the State GST would not be allowed except in the case of inter-State supply of goods.
5. The Centre and the States would have concurrent jurisdiction for the entire value chain and for all taxpayers on the basis of thresholds for goods and services prescribed by the States and the Centre.
6. The taxpayer would need to submit common format for periodical returns, to both the Central and to the concerned State GST authorities.
7. Each taxpayer would be allotted a PAN-linked taxpayer

identification number with a total of 13/15 digits.

8. Origin-based additional tax of 1 percent to be levied on inter-State supply of goods will be non-creditable in GST chain. The revenue from this tax is to be assigned to the origin State. This tax is proposed to be levied for an initial of two years or such period as recommended by the GST Council.
9. Entertainment tax, imposed by States on movies, theatres, etc. will be subsumed in the GST, but taxes on entertainment at panchayat, municipality or district level will continue.
10. Levy of GST on the newspapers and advertisements will give the government, access to substantial incremental revenues.
11. Stamp duties imposed on legal agreements by the State will continue to be levied by the States.
12. Abolition of entry tax/octroi across India.

Basic Structure of the GST

GST is a sales tax, which means it is a charge on the exchange (or "sale") of goods and services between individuals, businesses and organizations. As a sales tax, following are the basic elements that characterize the GST.

First, the GST is a *consumption sales tax*, which means that those who are purchasing the product, are responsible for paying the tax, as opposed to the "seller" of the product. For example, if we purchase a book from a bookstore, as a consumer, we are charged the GST in that particular transaction. This principle operates at all stages of production and distribution. Whenever a transaction occurs, be it at the manufacturing, distribution or retail stage, the party purchasing the good or service is required to pay the GST.

Second, it is a percentage consumption tax, which means that the amount of tax is based on a certain percentage of the sale cost (before taxes) of the good or service which we have purchased.

Third, the consumer pays the GST, while the seller or vendor is responsible for collecting and remitting the GST to the government. The consumer who purchases the book pays the GST to the bookstore and the bookstore remits it to the government at a later date. For example, in Canada, over the course of the tax year, vendors in Canada are responsible for keeping track of how much GST they have collected and then send that amount to the government.

GST as a Value Added Tax

Under the Canadian model, "The GST is a special sort of sales tax, commonly referred to as a value added sales tax. This type is distinctive in that it only taxes the monetary value added to a product at different stages of the production process. This is significant in that it overcomes the problem of cascading effects that can plague other sorts of sales tax. What exactly is a cascading effect? Consider a sales tax that is applied whenever a good or service exchanges hands. As such, a situation would occur in which the tax is applied multiple times in a product's life. Take, for example, a television. Firstly, the television must be made by a manufacturer, who purchases a number of inputs during the production process, such as raw materials and equipment. In purchasing these inputs, the manufacturer must pay a sales tax. This process continues through the wholesaling and retail stages. When a wholesaler purchases the television from the manufacturer, they have to pay tax in that transaction. When the retailer purchases the television from the wholesaler, another tax charge is applied. Finally, when you purchase the television from your local retailer, you again are charged a tax" (Canada Revenue Agency, June 22, 2006).

Under the Indian conditions, the new tax system would bring most indirect taxes under a single taxation regime including various Central indirect taxes such as Central excise duty, service tax, countervailing duty, as well as State value added tax (VAT), luxury tax, octroi and entry tax. This would lead to broadening of the tax base and increase in tax compliance, which could boost the economy every year in a sufficient manner. The GST is expected to reduce economic distortions caused by inter-State variations in taxes by including most indirect taxes under a single taxation regime. This could be achieved by addressing the bottlenecks of the value added tax (VAT) regime, which is in existence since 1986. (VAT was introduced for Central excise duty in 1986—first as MODVAT and then as CENVAT) to end the earlier "tax on tax" regime where the tax on the input was subject to taxation again at the output level on each intermediate goods in the manufacturing process.

Since VAT regulations and rates generally varied across States and different sectors, the need for GST arose to ensure uniform supply of goods and services across the country so that no additional taxes were required to be paid across different States as is prevalent today.

Yet, GST, too, has some inherent problems such as the division of taxation powers between the Central government and States. At present, the States cannot impose service tax while the Centre cannot levy tax on goods beyond the factory gate. A mutually agreeable formula for such a division between the Centre and the States had to be worked out. In the words of Professor Kavita Rao (National Institute of Public finance and Policy), the fixing of rates for both CGST and SGST will be administered by the GST Council and consequently the individual States will lose their right to tax whichever commodities they want at their specific interest. Economist Prabhat Patnaik pointed out that States will be alienated from their limited autonomy of taxing—like in the case of sales tax which accounted for 80 percent of their revenue (Sampant, 2015). Thus, the roadmap for GST to stand in compliance with fiscal federalism and co-operative federalism needs streamlining of the existing tax architecture instead of creating a new one.

Political Status of GST

For the first time, in 2006-07 Union Budget Speech the effort to introduce the new tax regime was reflected by the then Finance Minister Mr. P. Chidambaram who remarked, "there is a large consensus that the country must move towards a national level GST that must be shared between the Centre and the States. He proposed April 1, 2010 as the date for introducing the GST. The present rates for service tax and CENVAT, that is most proximate to the global GST rate, and the continuous steps towards phasing out of Central sales tax (CST), clearly hints at the endeavour on the part of Government of India".

Subsequently, the Empowered Committee of State Finance Ministers agreed to work with the Central Government to prepare a roadmap for introducing a national level GST with effect from April 1, 2010. In May 2007, the Empowered Committee (EC) of State Finance Ministers in consultation with the Central Government, constituted a Joint Working Group (JWG), to recommend the GST model.

On the completion of the first year of the Narendra Modi government at the Centre, the Union Finance Minister Arun Jaitley was upbeat about creating history, he addressed to the media on May 22 and opined, "We are in the process of creating history by bringing about the most important indirect tax reform—the GST (Goods and Services Tax)".

However, the government's plans of creating history went awry because of the logjam in the 2015 monsoon session of Parliament due to 'Lalit-gate' and 'Vyapam' scams.

The delay in the implementation of GST threatened to derail the reform process in no uncertain terms. The Government had set the April 1, 2016 deadline to roll out the GST regime but during the Budget Session of 2016 it could not be passed because of lack of majority in the Upper House and some reservation of the opposition parties—they wanted some amendment to the existing Bill.

Therefore, the monsoon session of the Parliament ended in

a virtual washout on August 13 with the government failing to get the GST Bill passed.

The Cabinet Committee on Parliamentary Affairs decided not to prorogue the session as yet and the House was adjourned sine die. This meant that a special session of the Parliament could be convened at a short notice to get the GST Bill approved by the Rajya Sabha.

On May 6, 2015, the Lok Sabha, where the ruling Bharatiya Janata Party-led National Democratic Alliance enjoys majority, had already passed the GST bill, officially named as the Constitution (One Hundred and Twenty-Second Amendment) Bill, 2014. (The Bill was introduced in the Lok Sabha on December 19, 2014 by Finance Minister Arun Jaitley after an earlier bill on GST—the Constitution (115th Amendment) Bill, 2011 introduced by the then Congress-led United Progressive Alliance government in the Parliament to enable the levy of GST in 2011, lapsed with the dissolution of the 15th Lok Sabha).

However, finally, the Rajya Sabha passed the Bill with 9 amendments on August 3, 2016 and the Lok Sabha passed the modified Bill on August 8, 2016, approving all the 9 amendments made by the Rajya Sabha.

This highlights the political aspects of the GST and explains why despite being passed in the Lok Sabha on May 6, 2015, the GST Bill was referred to a Select Committee of Rajya Sabha on May 14, 2015. This also explains the dissent notes from the Congress, the All India Anna Dravida Munnetra Kazhagham and Left parties on the report of the Rajya Sabha Select Committee that was tabled in Parliament in July 2015.

The GST Bill can only be implemented by a Constitutional amendment that means it is required to be passed by each House with at least two-thirds votes. Besides, there is no provision for a joint sitting of both the Houses in case of disagreement between the two Houses over the Constitutional Amendment Bill. There is no other way to pass any Constitutional amendment bill. This implies that to get the bill passed in the Rajya Sabha, the government required the support of at least 163 members. However, during the recent Upper House members' election, the NDA gained few more seats while the Congress lost some seats, making it a bit easier for the NDA to push the Bill.

This explains the whole story of politically driven bargaining and political innuendos. Stung by criticisms by the government that they derailed the reform process by not allowing the GST to be passed in the Rajya Sabha, the Congress members had hit back claiming it was the BJP that had delayed GST all these years—"Why (Prime Minister) Narendra Modi opposed the GST Bill when he was the Chief Minister of Gujarat?" The Communist Party of India (Marxist) went on put the blame on the government for stalling the Bill because the AIADMK was opposing the same—"The government needs their (the AIADMK's) support in the Parliament. Had they brought the GST bill then they would not have got the support".

As another deterrent to the passage of the Bill involved the Congress party's demands for a cap of 18 percent on GST, a dispute resolution authority and dropping of the 1 percent tax proposed inter-State trade or commerce. The main concerns of the Congress over the Bill included:

- 1 percent additional tax, as goods move across States.
- Constitutional cap of 18 percent and an independent dispute redressal mechanism.

The party has maintained that the government was ignoring the concerns raised by the Party on the legislation.

They want the Bill to be referred to a Select Committee for review.

Earlier all these demands were outright rejected by the government. The reasons being the following:

- The constitutional cap of 18 percent was not there in the Congress Bill that incorporated a Parliament Standing Committee's recommendation in 2013.
- The Congress had earlier accepted the formula that

disputes should be resolved in the GST Council which has one-third voting power with the Centre and two-thirds with the States and a three-fourths majority is required for any decision.

- Select Committee recommended that the 1 percent additional tax in its present form is likely to lead to "cascading of taxes".

But now the government has flexible attitude at this juncture and is trying to establish a unanimity.

Conclusion

The taxation of goods and services in India has, hitherto, been characterized as a cascading and distortionary tax on production, resulting in mis-allocation of resources and lower productivity and economic growth. It also inhibits voluntary compliance. It is well recognized that this problem can be effectively addressed by shifting the tax burden from production and trade to final consumption. A well designed destination-based value added tax on all goods and services is the most elegant method of eliminating distortions and taxing consumption. Sampant (2015) too had highlighted the political drawbacks in the model of the GST stating the federalism aspects. The model of GST will pose danger to federalism model where the regional actors won't be given due importance.

Under this structure, all different stages of production and distribution can be interpreted as a mere tax pass-through, and the tax essentially 'sticks' on final consumption within the taxing jurisdiction. The 'flawless' GST is designed as a consumption type destination VAT, based on invoice-credit method.

References

"Goods and Services Tax/Harmonized Sales Tax (GST/HST)", Canada Revenue Agency, June 22, 2006, available at: http://www.cra-arc.gc.ca/tax/business/topics/gst/menu-e.html.

"GST: An Overview of Some Alternatives", Government of Canada,

June 21, 2006, available at: http://dsp-psd.pwgsc.gc.ca/Collection-R/LoPBdP/.

"History of GST", available at: https://taxlane.in/2014/09/01/history-of-gst.

"Monsoon Session of Parliament Might Pass the GST Bill. What Does it Mean to You and Me?", available at: http://indiatoday.intoday.in/story/what-is-the-gst-what-are-salient-features-of-the-proposed-bill/1/533502.html.

Deepak, P. (2015), "Understanding the GST Bill Impasse", available at: http://www.elections.in/blog/understanding-the-gst-bill-impasse/#sthash.XtGqiB1Q.dpuf.

Sampant, G. (2015), "GST: Good for Business, Snag for Federalism", *The Hindu*.

19

GST: Administration and Implementation!

Premakumara G.S.

GST is a unique tax system applicable to the entire country and the Government has got the approval from the Parliament to implement it. Young researchers, particularly those working in the corporate world have positive opinion about GST and they are optimistic about GST.

I am of the opinion that now, we like it or not, the GST will be implemented in India. It is not only political or economical agenda; more appropriately, implementation of GST is an international obligation for India. Here, the question is, whether India is in the stage of sustaining the impacts of GST, and has it prepared and developed necessary pre-requisites to introduce the GST. Taking the examples from developed countries and from Europe is not appropriate. At the same time, the positive side of the GST cannot be denied.

The two important pre-requisites for implementation of GST are development of advanced information system and development of systematic supply chain system and very importantly, there is a need of combining these two systems; otherwise, there is a chance of corruption and misuse of the system. There is also a need for taking the confidence of State governments. If so, the negative aspects of the GST will be minimized and GST will immensely contribute in widening of the tax base, increase in tax revenue, reduction in the cost of tax and decrease in tax evasion—thereby the efficient GST will significantly contribute to the growth of the economy. Let us hope for the best and be optimistic about GST.

An important objective of tax reform is simplification of tax administration and compliance, which is dependent on three factors. The first determining factor for simplicity is the tax design itself. Generally, the more rational and neutral the tax design, the simpler it would be to administer and encourage compliance. If the tax is levied on a broad base at a single rate, there would be few classification disputes and the tax-specific record keeping requirements for vendors would be minimal. It would simplify enforce and encourage voluntary compliance.

The second factor is the infrastructure for tax administration, including the design of tax forms, data requirements, system of tax rulings and interpretations, and the procedures for registration, filing and processing of tax returns, tax payments and refunds, audits, and appeals. A modern tax administration focuses on providing services to taxpayers to facilitate compliance. It harnesses information technology to enhance the quality of services, and to ensure greater transparency in administration and enforcement.

The third factor in a federation such as India is the degree of harmonization among the taxes levied by the Centre and the States. The Empowered Committee has already indicated a preference for a dual GST, consisting of a Central GST and a State GST. Under this model, harmonization of the Central and State GSTs would be critical to keep the overall compliance burden low. Equally important is the harmonization of GST across the States.

Administration of GST

Keeping in mind the federal structure of India, there will be two components of GST—Central GST (CGST) and State GST (SGST). Both Centre and States will simultaneously levy GST across the value chain. Tax will be levied on every supply of goods and services. Centre would levy and collect Central goods and services tax (CGST), and States would levy and collect the State goods and services tax (SGST) on all transactions within a State. The input tax credit of CGST would be available for discharging the CGST liability on the output at each stage. Similarly, the credit of SGST paid on inputs would be allowed for paying the SGST on output. No cross utilization of credit would be permitted.

GST Council: The Constitutional Amendment Bill also seeks to empower the President to set up within 60 days of the passage of the legislation, a GST Council with the Union Finance Minister as chairperson and Union Minister of State for Revenue and Finance Ministers of all the States as members. The GST Council is to work on the basis of consensus and make recommendations on issues like GST rates, exemption lists, and threshold limits.

Further, the Bill provides for setting up of a GST dispute settlement authority, comprising a chairperson and two members to resolve disputes arising out of deviations from the recommendations of the GST Council either by the Central or State Governments. The draft Bill was referred to the Parliamentary Committee on Finance for examination.

Getting the design of the GST right is therefore critical. Specifically, the GST should aim at tax rates that protect revenue, simplify administration, encourage compliance, avoid adding to inflationary pressures, and keep India in the range of countries with reasonable levels of indirect taxes.

Choices that the GST Council makes regarding exemptions/low taxation (for example, on gold and precious metals, and area-based exemptions) will be critical. The more the exemptions that are retained, the higher will be the standard rate. There is no getting away from a simple and powerful reality: the broader the scope of exemptions, the less effective the GST will be. For example, if precious metals continue to enjoy highly concessional rates, the rest of the economy will have to pay in the form of higher rates on other goods, including the essential ones.

GST Network (GSTN): Among the other steps that are being taken for the introduction of GST is the establishment of a strong information technology (IT) infrastructure. For this purpose, the Government has set up an Empowered Group under the chairmanship of Mr. Nandan Nilekani. Significant progress has been made in the conceptualization and design of the GSTN—a common portal for the Centre and the States that will enable electronic processing of the key business processes of registration, returns, and payments. For this purpose, the structure of these processes is in advanced stages of finalization.

The National Securities Depository Limited (NSDL) has been selected as the technology partner for incubating the National Information Utility that will establish and operate the IT backbone for the GST. In this regard, the NSDL has set up a pilot project in collaboration with 11 States prior to its roll-out across the country. Three Joint Working Groups of officials have also been constituted comprising officials from the Central Government, State Governments, and an Empowered Committee of State Finance Ministers to work on legislation, business procedures and IT infrastructure respectively.

The structure of GSTN has been approved by the Empowered Committee of State Finance Ministers. GSTN will be set up as a National Information Utility. GSTN will implement common PAN-based registration, returns filing and payments processing for all States on a shared platform. The use of PAN as a common identifier in both direct and indirect taxes, will enhance transparency and check tax evasion.

Main Features of the Registration Procedures under GST: The major features of the proposed registration procedures under GST are as follows:

1. **Existing Dealers:** Existing VAT/Central excise/Service tax payers will not have to apply afresh for registration under the GST.
2. **New Dealers:** Single application to be filed online for registration under GST.
3. The registration number will be PAN-based and will serve the purpose for Centre and States.
4. Unified application to both tax authorities.

5. Each dealer to be given a unique ID GSTIN.
6. Deemed approval within three days.
7. Post-registration verification in risk based cases only.

Main Features of the Returns Filing Procedures under GST: The major features of the proposed returns filing procedures under GST are as follows:

1. Common return would serve the purpose of both Centre and State Governments.
2. There are eight forms provided for in the GST business processes for filing for returns. Most of the average tax payers would be using only four forms for filing their returns. These are return for supplies, return for purchases, monthly returns and annual return.
3. Small taxpayers: Small taxpayers who have opted composition scheme shall have to file return on quarterly basis.
4. Filing of returns shall be completely online. All taxes can also be paid online.

Main Features of the Payment Procedures under GST: The major features of the proposed payments procedures under GST are as follows:

1. Electronic payment process—no generation of paper at any stage.
2. Single point interface for challan generation—GSTN.
3. Ease of payment—payment can be made through online banking, credit card/debit card, NEFT/RTGS and through cheque/cash at the bank.
4. Common challan form with auto-population features.
5. Use of single challan and single payment instrument.
6. Common set of authorized banks.
7. Common accounting codes.

Implementation of GST

For nearly ten years, India has been on the verge of implementing GST. After the passage of the 122nd Constitutional Amendment Bill by the Lok Sabha and the

Rajya Sabha, the country is ready to execute one of the most ambitious and remarkable tax reforms in its post-Independence history. Implementing a new tax, encompassing both goods and services, by the Centre and the States in a large and complex federal system, is perhaps unprecedented in modern global tax history.

Lok Sabha passed the 122nd Constitutional Amendment—Goods and Services Tax Bill on May 6, 2015. Rajya Sabha passed the 122nd Constitutional Amendment Bill with 9 amendments on August 3, 2016. Lok Sabha passed the modified 122nd Constitution Amendment Bill on August 8, 2016 approving all the 9 amendments by the Rajya Sabha.

The Bill now requires clearance of at least half (15 out of the 29) of the States to be given the President's approval. And then both the Centre and States have to pass Central GST and State GST Bills respectively and rules have to be made under them. Currently, the hope is that GST will be implemented from April 1, 2017.

To sum up, as the world economy slows, and increasing financial volatility and turbulence become the *newest normal*, only a few economies have the resilience to be a refuge of stability and the potential to be an outpost of opportunity. India is one of those few. As oil and commodity prices continue to be soft, macroeconomic stability seems reasonably assured for India. This bedrock of stability coupled with reforms can propel the economy to a high growth trajectory. Key amongst these reforms is the national level GST.

The Indian GST is expected to represent a leap forward in creating a much cleaner dual VAT which would minimize the disadvantages of completely independent and completely centralized systems. A common base and common rates (across goods and services) and very similar rates (across States and between Centre and States) will facilitate administration and improve compliance while also rendering manageable the collection of taxes on inter-state sales. At the same time, the exceptions—in the form of permissible additional excise taxes on petroleum and tobacco for the Centre, and petroleum and alcohol for the States)—will provide the requisite fiscal autonomy to the States. Indeed, even if they are brought within the scope of the GST, the states will retain autonomy in being able to levy top-up taxes on these goods.